FAMILY FAVORITES
MADE HEALTHY

Health & Wellness Cooking Library™

Cover Designer: Julie Cisler

Interior Designer: Tanja Lipinski Cole

ISBN 1–57954–762–1

2   4   6   8   10   9   7   5   3   1   hardcover

National Health & Wellness Club
12301 Whitewater Drive
Minnetonka, MN 55343
www.healthandwellnessclub.com

contents

chapter 1

Healthy Habits— Now and Forever

THE FAT-FIGHTING EDGE

America is the land of plenty—plenty of burgers, plenty of pizza, plenty of apple pie. The result for too many of us is extra pounds that sap our energy and threaten our health. Clearly, the excess weight has to go, but getting rid of it is never easy. Even when you are successful, those unwanted pounds have a way of picking up your scent like a pack of bloodhounds hot on your trail. Before you know it, they've once again got you surrounded.

So how do you lose those dogs—er, pounds—once and for all? You have to change your scent. Become a new person. Become a person who no longer leads an overweight lifestyle with its overweight habits. And the trick is to do it without taxing your willpower, without subjecting yourself to undue deprivation and without adding rules and regulations that you can't wait to be rid of.

In other words, you have to create a new lifestyle that you can follow long enough to have it become second nature. You want a friend that hangs around for the rest of your life, guarding you against ever gaining weight again.

Understand the Basics

Does the phrase "look before you leap" ring a bell? You can't make an honest commitment to do something unless you have some idea of what is required. So let's go through the healthy-lifestyle facts of life.

The first fact of life is that you can't lose 30 pounds in a month. Nor would you want to. After all, the goal isn't just to lose weight; it's to keep the pounds off permanently. And most experts agree that you have the best chances of doing that if you take a gradual approach—dropping no more than one pound a week.

The second fact of life is that in order to lose that pound a week, you need to establish a daily deficit of 500 calories. That requires some combination of the right foods and the right exercise. Most weight-loss experts favor a program in which you cut 200 calories of fat (roughly 22 grams of fat) from your daily diet and burn off 300 calories through exercise to achieve the magic number. (When it comes to diet, it's actually better to count grams of fat instead of calories.)

The third fact of life is that the first two facts are useless unless you follow them consistently and maintain them long after excess pounds are gone. That means being comfortable with the changes you make and not demanding more of yourself than you are prepared to give.

Fat Facts

The average American's diet is approximately 40 percent fat. And because fat calories are more readily converted into body fat, those kinds of calories are the first ones you want to reduce. But the question is, by how much?

Diet experts advocate a fat intake of no more than 25 percent of total calories. What does that really mean? Well, for a woman to maintain a weight of 130 pounds, for instance, she should take in about 1,600 calories a day. If only 25 percent of those calories come from fat, that's 400 calories' worth. Since each gram of fat is good for 9 calories, that's an upper level of 44 grams of fat a day. If you are a 160-pound woman eating 2,000 calories a day (at the 40 percent fat level), you're currently consuming about 89 grams of fat. To reach a streamlined 130 pounds, you need to figure out how to be satisfied with 45 fewer grams of fat per day. But not all at once.

As we mentioned before, to jump onto the pound-a-week weight-loss wagon, you need to cut 500 calories a day: 200 from your daily intake and 300 through exercise. With exercise making its hefty contribution, all that is really required to get the weight-loss wagon rolling is that you bid farewell to approximately 22 grams of fat per day.

After a certain amount of time, your 22-gram fat deficit, along with exercise, can slim your body to a point where it functions so efficiently that you stop losing weight. At this point, having become used to the dietary changes you've made, you can then go ahead and cut your fat intake far enough to reach a fat budget that corresponds to your dream maintenance weight.

While sheer instinct may tell you to grit your teeth and cut all the fat in sight, hoping your willpower holds out, that is the last thing you should do. "Completely eliminating your problem foods may set you up for failure," says Judith S. Stern, Sc.D., professor of nutrition and internal medicine at the University of California, Davis. "You have to determine what those foods are and find ways to replace them if you can't control your appetite for them."

Diane Hanson, Ph.D., a lifestyle specialist at the Pritikin Longevity Center in Santa Monica, California, thinks of it as leveraging your food choices: "Doable changes that make a big difference. For example, if two or three tablespoons of blue-cheese dressing at lunch are dumping 16 or 24 grams of fat onto your daily intake, a small packet of low-fat dressing brought from home can shave off the grams and still leave you satisfied."

The concept of food substitutes is nothing new. But what makes them so exciting now is the ever-growing selection of low-fat products that are on the market. The difference between a regular meat lasagna entrée and a low-fat one translates into a fat savings of 7 grams. A nonfat, fruit-filled breakfast pastry can save you 16 grams of fat if you substitute it for the "real thing." Suddenly, dropping your fat intake for life doesn't look like such hungry work. But whatever you drop should be dropped for good. So choose carefully, or the pounds will return.

Before you lull yourself to sleep with visions of breakfast-pastry weight loss, remember this: At some point, you're going to have to sweat. A study conducted by Dr. Susan Kayman, Dr. William Bruvold and Dr. Judith Stern at the University of California found that 90 percent of the participants who kept the weight off exercised regularly.

The Exercise Equation

"To my mind, exercise has been undervalued with respect to weight loss," says Dr. Hanson. "As a matter of fact, when you look at what determines the continuation of a healthy lifestyle, exercise turns out to be the biggest behavioral driver."

It helps you look good and feel even better. It gives you a sense of accomplishment and mastery over your situation. "Research is even showing that exercise may enhance your preference for fruits and vegetables," says Dr. Hanson.

Even if you already like veggies, exercise serves another important purpose. When you lower your calorie intake, your body, with an instinct for survival, slows down its metabolic rate and conserves energy. Exercise turns up the furnace so you become more efficient at burning fat. And to drop a pound a week, you want that furnace stoked to the tune of 300 calories burned a day.

How you accomplish that goal is a matter of what you like to do. But the good news is that even a brisk 45-minute walk will do the trick. But the real trick is to do it every day.

Make the Commitment

The difference between losing weight and losing weight for good is commitment: a truly motivated desire not only to change but also to maintain that change. You can think of your commitment as a lifetime contract with yourself. Of course, we've all cheated on some of our vows to become better, more effective or slimmer. In most cases, the problem isn't our willpower but our initial commitment. It just wasn't strong enough.

Before starting your new, lighter life, you need to make sure that you're revved and ready to do it and that the contract you make with yourself is so strong that the Supreme Court—or a tempting éclair with your name on it—couldn't break it. Here's how to really, pardon the expression, commit yourself.

Choose the right moment. "It's not easy to begin a program during complicated periods in your life," says Kelly D. Brownell, Ph.D., professor of psychology at Yale University. "Divorce, an illness in the family, problems at work—those are all things that can sap your energy and make your environment less supportive for the changes you want to make."

Of course, some people thrive on complications. A divorce, for example, may be just the motivating kick one person needs to make big changes as part of a whole new lifestyle. "The thing you need to consider," says Dr. Brownell, "is how you respond to complications. If stress, worry and a frantic pace erode your eating plan, making serious lifestyle changes in the midst of what's currently happening may be a mistake."

And you don't want to look just at the present. If you're due for "stormy weather" in the upcoming weeks and months, you may want to bide your time and embark on your new lifestyle once things calm down and the sun comes out again.

Choose the right commitment. Do you want to lose a certain number of pounds, or do you want to lose the bad habits that made you overweight to begin with? While those two goals may seem to be heads and tails of the same coin, the side that lands up after the toss can make all the difference between pounds gone forever and pounds gone for an all-too-brief amount of time.

"If you find yourself fantasizing about the moment when you've lost the weight and your diet is over, you're going to have problems," says Dr. Brownell. "At the point when you've finally reached that all-important number on the scale, there's a chance that your motivation to continue your healthy lifestyle may decrease, leaving you right back where you started."

So to make the commitment that will keep those pounds away forever, focus on the changes you plan to make. "Change your view of success," suggests Dr. Hanson. "Rather than making weight loss your goal, make life-long health your goal. Rather than getting up each morning and heading for the scale, wake up and notice how much better you feel."

"I also find it helpful to think of overweight as a chronic condition," adds Dr. Brownell. "Just as diabetes requires constant maintenance lest it get serious, maintaining your ideal weight requires a lifetime of healthy eating and exercising practices."

Choose the right reason. "Some people lose weight because their husbands or wives want them to," says Jerome Brandon, Ph.D., an exercise physiologist from Georgia State University in Atlanta and member of the American College of Sports Medicine. "The problem is that they make the effort to lose weight for someone else rather than because they themselves are personally motivated to do it. And eventually, they will get tired of doing it."

So do it for yourself and not for someone else.

Get Prepared

Every great journey begins with a great deal of preparation. How far would Christopher Columbus have gotten if he'd just awakened one morning, kissed his wife and headed out to discover the New World without the proper clothes, food, transportation or navigational equipment?

Changing your life is not much different from making a journey. In both cases, the most disappointing thing that can happen is that you have to give up because of difficulties you weren't prepared for. So no matter how charged up you are to start your new life, take some time to make the following preparations.

Educate yourself. If you're going to make lifestyle changes that you expect to practice for the rest of your life, you'd darn well better believe in them. And the best way to believe in something is to know beyond a shadow of a doubt how it works and, more important, why it works.

"First, when it comes to weight loss, there are scientific reasons for why it's best to eat and exercise a certain way," says Dr. Hanson. "If you understand how your body is designed to work, you'll believe in what you're doing and not be so inclined to give it up when the results are not happening as quickly as you want."

Second, by not understanding their body's own weight-loss mechanisms, people often select popular methods that doom them to failure. Then they blame themselves—when they never really had a chance. "You may think that the more calories you deprive yourself of, the faster you'll lose weight, and that's initially true. But if you don't realize that the body slows down its fat-burning furnace when calories are suddenly reduced, you're ultimately in for a big disappointment," says Dr. Hanson. "The only thing that will happen over time is that you'll be hungrier, less inclined to continue your program and still not sure why you aren't maintaining the initial weight loss."

So start out right by getting the facts. Know without a doubt that what you are doing is right and will eventually provide you with the results you want regardless of how things appear to be going on a day-to-day basis.

Find substitutes for eating. "When talking to patients, I often ask them why they overeat, why are they doing something that they know is ultimately harmful," says Dean Ornish, M.D., director of the Preventive Medicine Research Institute in Sausalito, California, and author of the best-selling *Eat More, Weigh Less*. "And the answer often is that it helps to get them through the day. They may feel alienated or isolated, and eating helps them deal with the pain. One patient described how food temporarily fills the void and numbs the pain."

According to Dr. Ornish, change is not brought about solely by focusing on new behaviors such as changing your eating habits and exercising. You need to address the underlying reasons for your behaviors. Otherwise, the problem remains and will eventually sabotage all your good intentions and commitments.

If some form of mental stress is behind your eating problem, you'll need to find a nonfattening substitute. Relaxation techniques and spending more time with friends are both great alternatives that are far lower in calories than a banana split.

Remove roadblocks. Visualize the changes you want to make, then visualize all the things that could keep you from doing them. "It could be that you are unwilling to start exercising," says Dr. Brownell. "But if you dig a little deeper, you may find that the reason is that you are embarrassed to be seen exercising."

If that is the case, then starting your new lifestyle by taking out a membership at the trendy new health club that everyone is going to would probably be a mistake. That membership card will get about as much use as a coupon good for five free wrestling lessons.

Instead, acknowledge your fear and create an environment that guarantees privacy—maybe a stationary bike in your bedroom or an early-morning walk.

The same thing goes for food. If you know in your heart of hearts that you will never give up apple pie, then don't say you will and set yourself up for failure. Create a new recipe that makes apple pie less fattening.

Get support. "If you look at the factors that predict successful, permanent weight loss, social support ranks near the top of the list," says John Foreyt, Ph.D., director of the Nutrition Research Clinic at Baylor College of Medicine in Houston and co-author of *Living without Dieting.* "I'd go so far as to say that it is absolutely critical."

When starting your new lifestyle, Dr. Foreyt insists that you make a public commitment, but not for the normal reasons. "It's not that you want to force yourself into a situation you can't back down from because everyone knows about it. What you are actually doing is making an assertive appeal for people's help and understanding."

In his book, Dr. Foreyt outlines four levels of support, each with its own special purpose. "First there's your family. They're going to need to get used to your new lifestyle. It may be that certain foods have to be kept out of the house. Compromises on family time may need to be made when your exercise or other activities conflict with family plans."

The second level is composed of close friends. "Everyone should have someone they can call when temptation rears its ugly head," says Dr. Foreyt. "Even one really good friend can make the difference in a crisis."

The third and fourth levels involve support groups and your doctor. "Support groups are the perfect place to get advice and encouragement from people experiencing the same things you are," notes Dr. Foreyt. "And your doctor gives you information and feedback and helps you monitor your progress."

For some people, maintaining all four levels of support is not necessary.

But Dr. Foreyt still maintains the need for some form of social support, even for loners. And more important, the kind of support you solicit needs to be specific.

"You don't want people giving you negative support," says Dr. Foreyt. "While someone pointing out your mistakes may work in the short run, it isn't motivating over the long haul. So you want to be very direct about asking people to say something positive about your accomplishments."

Find a monitoring system that works. "Your actual weight is the least important thing you can monitor," says Ronette Kolotkin, Ph.D., director of behavioral programs at Duke University's Diet and Fitness Center and co-author of *The Duke University Medical Center Book of Diet and Fitness.* "Instead, I always encourage people to keep a diary not just of food and exercise but also of any important behavioral problems they encounter, such as rapid eating in certain situations or a tendency to binge at particular times."

At the end of each week, Dr. Kolotkin suggests, study your diary as if you were a weight-loss professional studying someone else's case history. What advice would you give the patient? A one-year follow-up study conducted by Dr. Kolotkin found that people who monitored food intake, exercise and motivation were more successful than those who monitored weight only.

Paying daily homage to the bathroom scale is a dicey proposition for two reasons. First, your body weight is in constant flux. Up a pound today, down two tomorrow. A momentary gain in water weight may have you on the floor in despair despite the fact that the overall picture is improving.

Second, because your new lifestyle of healthy food and exercise is constantly trimming the fat while boosting the lean, a scale may show no change in weight even though you are getting slimmer and more toned by the minute. "That's why I always encourage people to wear form-fitting clothing," says Dr. Kolotkin. "As you lose weight or even as your body composition changes, you'll get feedback every time you need to have your clothes taken in a bit. You'll constantly be aware of what your body is doing by the way your clothes fit."

Plan for trouble. "I always tell people that they can expect to slip," says Dr. Kolotkin. "It will happen. And the difference between moving on and just plain giving up has to do with having some strategy to deal with momentary failure."

There are two ways you don't want to react to a temporary backslide. On one hand, you don't want to be cavalier: "Oh well, I ate that box of doughnuts, but I'll worry about it tomorrow." On the other hand, you don't want to overreact: "Oh no, this is the end! How can I go on after eating my weight in doughnuts? I'm no good."

"You have to be rational," says Dr. Kolotkin. "The first thing to do is acknowledge exactly what happened. 'I was at a party, lost control and ate 5,000 calories.' Don't overemphasize or underemphasize what occurred. Next, put it into perspective. 'Over the past six months, I've made some great changes; I've exercised regularly, eaten right and made serious progress. Compared with what I've achieved, this one incident is hardly a catastrophe. I don't feel great about it, but it isn't the end of the world.'"

Next comes action. A good general doesn't waste time dwelling on defeat. Instead, he immediately plots a course of action that will take him back on the road to victory. "That does not mean you should exercise twice as long tomorrow to make up for today's mistake," says Dr. Kolotkin. "That's a lot like punishing yourself. Instead, you want to take steps to ensure that what happened does not happen again."

If you found yourself bingeing on a bag of chips lying wantonly open in the kitchen, you may want to purge your house of binge foods. If you stopped exercising for a week because of scheduling difficulties, spend some time arranging things so that it doesn't happen again. "Then get right back into your program," says Dr. Kolotkin. "Set two alarm clocks so that you can't avoid waking up and exercising. Meet a friend for lunch who will make sure you eat the right foods. Write out a meal plan."

In other words, make your lifestyle changes foolproof and inescapable for the next few days just to get yourself back on track. Dr. Kolotkin finds that it takes most people only three days to turn around a negative incident.

Learn from past mistakes. What went wrong the last time you tried to lose weight? "When I ask people that, I'll normally get an unproductive answer like they started eating again," says Dr. Kolotkin. "But you need to look at the underlying reasons. Was the diet you placed yourself on too restrictive? Did you find that your meal plans were falling apart because you were often pressed for time and had to eat whatever was available?" Take some time to dig deep and honestly analyze what went wrong.

Create an environment that makes change easy. Weight loss and lifestyle change are so often looked at as matters of sheer willpower. But why make things tough when you can make them easy? "I call it environmental engineering," says Dr. Hanson, "and it's really where you make changes in your environment that make it easier to succeed."

Environmental engineering is a powerful yet simple concept. If you find yourself getting hungry at 3:00 each afternoon and the only thing available is a candy machine down the hall from your office, don't put yourself in the position of having to fight the urge to merge with a chocolate bar. Instead, reach into your desk and pull out the apple that you brought along for just such a moment.

That idea can be applied to all areas of your life. And once you've determined why you've failed in the past, you can set up your new environment to help avoid past mistakes. "When I encounter people who have a problem with after-dinner eating, I often suggest that they get a small refrigerator for beverages and keep it in the den," says Dr. Kolotkin. "That way, even if they are thirsty, they don't need to enter the kitchen and be tempted by an open refrigerator."

As for exercise, did your last walking program peter out after a week because you never seemed to have clean socks, batteries for your personal stereo or rain gear? Get equipped. Keep everything where you can get at it immediately. Keep an extra pair of walking shoes in your car for impromptu opportunities. Make it so easy on yourself that you can't possibly fail.

Take Action

You're ready to get started. But at what pace? Do you purge all the fat from your diet, change your eating habits and throw yourself into a daily exercise program in one fell swoop? Or should you ease into a lifestyle change like you ease into a hot tub—making a few food substitutions, exercising a couple days a week, getting comfortable?

When making your decision, don't think about how fast you want to lose weight. The real question is which technique makes it easier to assimilate changes that you can keep for life.

"If you're looking to make permanent lifestyle changes, my feeling is that incorporating them slowly makes them easier to get used to," says Dr. Kolotkin. "It's less overwhelming. The goals seem more attainable if you go step-by-step rather than full force."

Dr. Kolotkin experienced the power of small changes firsthand in working with a woman who, at age 45, had never exercised and was so out of shape that a flight of stairs would leave her winded and grasping the banister for support. When she started her program, five minutes on a stationary bike was all she could do. "But rather than dwell on the thought that five minutes was not a very big or important change, she embraced the notion of small, gradual changes and took pride in the fact that she was actually exercising at all," says Dr. Kolotkin. "And gradually, over the following months, as she got comfortable with one level of exercise, she increased it. She has now been in four walking marathons!"

Of course, Dr. Kolotkin is quick to admit that gradual change means gradual results, sometimes too gradual for some people. "It's not as exciting or motivating to make small changes, so some people resist it, thinking that they'll never get where they want to be. "But then I remind them that they tried cutting calories too quickly in the past and found the diet too restrictive to continue. Although they did lose some fast weight, in the end, they went back to their old habits and gained it back."

On the other hand, if you like big, exciting changes, you have an ally in Dr. Ornish. According to him, comprehensive changes can make people feel so much better so quickly that, rather than being overwhelmed by the changes, they are instead strongly motivated to continue.

So which is right for you? Part of the answer lies with your doctor and your current situation. Big dietary changes may be within your capability, but if you haven't been exercising regularly, too much activity too fast could be dangerous.

The second part of the answer has to do with your own mental makeup. Do big challenges bring out the best in you or do you find them intimidating? What has worked for you in other situations? Remember, the only right answer here is the one that's right for you.

Best Bets for Health Watchers

EATING LIGHT IN THE REAL WORLD

You're cruising down the interstate when breakfast beckons. It's fast food or nothing, but can you refuel on such fare without taking a detour around your healthy diet?

You're cooling your heels at the airport between flights. Hunger strikes as you catch a whiff of just-baked cookies. A transgression can send you into a tailspin, but can you resist?

Situations like these can be challenging for health-conscious people. But no matter how difficult a situation, choices are usually available—some better than others.

The key in these circumstances is to make choices actively, not passively, says Sachiko St. Jeor, Ph.D., professor of nutrition at the University of Nevada School of Medicine in Reno. "You don't have to be a victim of your environment," Dr. St. Jeor says. "You can take control."

With those words of inspiration in mind, we decided to explore some real diet danger zones to find the best choices. Here are some ideas that may help you make informed food choices in any situation.

Fast-Food Breakfast

GOOD: Pancakes

A decent choice in any fast-food restaurant, assuming you hold the butter or margarine and go easy on the syrup. At Hardee's, which offers the most diet-friendly pancakes by fast-food standards, three pancakes contain 280 calories and just 2 grams of fat (6 percent of calories). McDonald's pancakes aren't bad either, with 245 calories and 4 grams fat (15 percent of calories) in three.

BETTER: McDonald's fat-free apple bran muffin

Only 180 calories, no fat. Add a glass of orange juice (about 60 calories and no fat in 6 ounces) and 8 ounces of 1 percent milk (about 110 calories and 2 grams fat) and you have a pretty nutritious, low-fat breakfast for 350 calories, says Dr. St. Jeor.

BEST: A bowl of nonsugary cereal

McDonald's serves up Cheerios (¾ cup for 80 calories and 1 gram fat) and Wheaties (¾ cup for 90 calories and 1 gram fat)—either of which provides about 15 to 30 percent of the daily quota for iron and vitamins A and C. Pour on the 1 percent milk and the total calorie count is still under 200—plus you meet about a third of your daily calcium requirement.

Fast-Food Chicken Sandwiches

GOOD: Arby's Lite Roast Chicken Deluxe or Wendy's Grilled Chicken Sandwich

Here are two sandwiches worth clucking about. Arby's has 276 calories and 7 grams fat (23 percent of calories). Wendy's chicken sandwich is close, with 290 calories and 7 grams fat (22 percent of calories).

BETTER: Chick-Fil-A Chargrilled Chicken Sandwich

This East Coast chain offers one lean chicken, with just 17 percent of calories from fat (258 calories, 4.8 grams fat). If you have high blood pressure, however, take note: This sandwich may be low in fat, but it's high in sodium, with 1,121 milligrams.

BEWARE: All others

A chicken sandwich by any other name could be a fat trap. Burger King's Chicken Sandwich, for example, will set you back 700 calories, with 54 percent of those calories from fat. McDonald's McChicken (470 calories and 25 grams fat), Wendy's Breaded Chicken (450 calories, 20 grams fat) and Arby's Grilled Chicken Deluxe (430 calories, 19.9 grams fat) aren't much better, with 40 to 48 percent of calories from fat.

Cinema Fare

OKAY: Red licorice

Red Vines, for example, by American Licorice Company, has only 140 calories and no fat in seven licorice sticks. Trouble is, we're talking empty calories here; red licorice has virtually no nutrient value.

BETTER: Nonbuttered popcorn

Only 55 calories, about 100 milligrams sodium and about 3.1 grams fat per cup for oil-popped corn. The problem is, who can stop at a cup? Most theaters serve up popcorn by the gallon, which makes fat, calorie and sodium totals soar.

BEST: Eat before the film

"Remind yourself that movies last just two hours, and you can go that long without food," says Dr. St. Jeor. "Get into watching the movie as a pure experience, without shoveling down food you can't see or really enjoy."

Midafternoon Snacks

GOOD: Low-fat, low-sugar dried cereal

Cheerios or mini shredded wheat will do. These cereals are not just low in fat but also nutrient-fortified.

ALSO GOOD: Prunes

Seven prunes contain about 140 calories, no fat and 4 grams of dietary fiber.

BEST: Instant bean soup

Packaged in individual serving cups—and available in a wide variety of flavors—instant bean soups are easy to take to the office. Just add boiling water or add cold water and heat in the microwave. Two good choices are a black bean soup made by Fantastic Foods and a couscous tomato minestrone made by Nile Spice. Both are rich and tasty—and can really satisfy an appetite for about 200 calories and 1 gram or less of fat. Nutritionist Evelyn Tribole, R.D., author of *Healthy Homestyle Cooking*, points out that many such soups are high in vitamins (including C and A), minerals like iron, complex carbohydrates and fiber.

Airport Food

GOOD: Sushi

It's becoming as all-American as bagels. In airports, stick with the kind with the cooked fish filling (like those with crabmeat) or vegetable filling to avoid risk of parasites, says Judith S. Stern, Sc.D., professor of nutrition and internal medicine at the University of California, Davis. A full serving of vegetable sushi contains about 365 calories and just 1 gram of fat.

BETTER: Nonfat frozen yogurt

Four ounces of Honey Hill Farms Ghirardelli Chocolate flavor, for example, contains 115 calories, no fat and, as a bonus, 110 milligrams of calcium—a boon for the bones. (Skip the "mix-ins" like chopped candy and nuts.)

EVEN BETTER: A steaming cup of decaf café latte (made with skim milk)

A café latte is mostly hot milk, with a little espresso floated on top. You sate your appetite and do your bones a calcium favor (264 milligrams in 7 ounces for less than 80 calories and less than half a gram of fat).

BEST: Take a fitness walk through the terminal

You can chart your course and ensure that you don't get lost by picking up a map of the terminal at the information desk. Tip: Wear a fanny pack or backpack so you can stride more freely in your travels.

Airplane Meals and Snacks

GOOD: Pasta entrées

Meat entrées are usually greasy, notes Dr. Stern, while pasta entrées are generally lower in fat.

BETTER: Fly American Airlines

They're starting to routinely offer Weight Watchers frozen meals—the same kind you get in the supermarket—on many flights, without advance reservations.

BEST: Plan ahead

Don't leave your in-flight food up to chance. Pack snack food—like fruit, a bagel or serving-size cereal—in your carry-on bag so you won't be tempted by the salted peanuts or smoked almonds, suggests John Foreyt, Ph.D., director of the Nutrition Research Clinic at Baylor College of Medicine in Houston and co-author of *Living without Dieting.* And don't forget to order a special low-fat meal in advance. A low-fat, low-cholesterol breakfast on United Airlines, for example, might include fresh fruit, an asparagus and egg-substitute frittata, mushroom ragout and a roasted tomato half. Talk about friendly skies!

Finally, drink lots of bottled water. It keeps you hydrated and reduces your appetite.

Mixed Drinks

GOOD: Virgin (nonalcoholic) fresh-fruit daiquiris

A daiquiri has about 80 to 100 calories, with little or no fat. The standard recipe calls for about half a cup of fresh fruit (like strawberries, which contain roughly 30 calories), 2 ounces of a mixer called sweet-and-sour (a nonfat lemon-and-sugar drink, with about 50 calories) and a big scoop of ice.

BEST: Virgin Mary

This spicy tomato-juice concoction is a boon in so many ways. It fills you with liquid; it's low-cal—about 32 calories for a 6-ounce glass; it's nonfat; it's spicy, which satisfies tastebuds; it provides some nutrition in the form of vitamin C; and finally, there's a great big celery stick to provide crunch appeal.

Burgers in Disneyland

GOOD: Turkey burger

Served with lettuce, tomato and fat-free Thousand Island dressing on a honey wheat bun, it contains only 367 calories and 9.5 grams fat (23 percent of calories).

BEST: Veggie burger

This burger has the same fat-free dressing and bun as the turkey burger, with only 365 calories and 8 grams fat (19 percent of calories).

Ballpark Fare

GOOD: Check out the latest offerings

It's a whole new ball game out there. Stadium concessionaires are innovating to appeal to the increasing numbers of female sports fans, says Matthew Bauer, media manager for Sportservice Corporation in Buffalo, the leading food supplier to ballparks across the country. Among the new offerings:

- Rotisserie chicken, as an alternative to fried chicken, available at The Ballpark in Arlington, which is home to the Texas Rangers. (A great choice, as long as you remove the skin.) Also in several parks: grilled chicken served on a bed of greens.

- The vegetarian burrito at Tiger Stadium in Detroit—loaded with julienned strips of zucchini, peppers and onions in a soft flour tortilla.

- Fresh sliced-turkey sandwiches at Dodger Stadium in Los Angeles and other locales.

- Frozen-fruit pops and low-fat frozen yogurt, available at Sportservice client stadiums, including Riverfront Stadium in Cincinnati, Comiskey Park in Chicago, Busch Stadium in St. Louis and the Gateway sports complex in Cleveland.

BEST: Crudités

At Dodger Stadium, they give it a more manly name (relish tray), but that's what it is—a plate loaded with fresh cucumbers, celery, carrots and radishes.

BEWARE: Ordering from your seat

A less-fortunate new trend in stadium cuisine is the legion of waiters sent out with handheld computers who take your order at your seat and then deliver the food to you. Just say no! Stand up and go get it yourself: Walking burns calories.

Chinese Meals

GOOD: A shared entrée of stir-fried vegetables and lots of steamed rice

Chinese-food lovers reeled in shock when news stories revealed that many of their favorite dishes are loaded with fatty oils. And it's true: A typical serving of stir-fried veggies can contain 400 calories and anywhere from 6 to 18 grams of fat. But you can avoid some of the fat and still enjoy this flavorful cuisine by sharing an entrée. To appease your appetite, pile on the steamed rice.

BEST: Steamed veggies with chicken or shrimp

Even if it's not on the menu, most cooks in Chinese restaurants can create a delectable steamed meal. Often, they serve it in a beautiful bamboo steamer. For flavor, sprinkle the food with soy sauce or ask for a brown sauce with scallions on the side to drizzle on top. In these entrées, light-meat chicken contains only about 175 calories and 5 grams fat, while shrimp is even leaner, with only about 85 calories and less than 1 gram of fat.

Restaurant Desserts

GOOD: Two forks

Share whatever dessert you order with a friend. "If you're used to eating dessert and you let yourself have just a bite or two, you'll be less likely to feel deprived and binge later," says Dr. Foreyt.

BETTER: Decaf cappuccino (espresso with frothed skim milk)

Tribole suggests having it with a biscotti or two on the side. Many different companies manufacture biscotti—almond cookies designed for dipping. They're generally low in fat and calories. Some biscotti have only 30 calories and less than 1 gram of fat per cookie.

BEST: Sorbet

This tangy juice-based dessert is mostly water. A half-cup of fruit sorbet, such as pineapple or peach, might provide about 120 calories and no fat.

Chocolate Lovers' Supermarket Snacks

GOOD: Snackwell's Devil's Food Cookie Cakes

Deep, chocolate, cakey interior surrounded by a thin layer of marshmallow, then a dark chocolate coating—so sweet and rich, it's hard to believe they're fat-free. Drawbacks: Each hefty cookie contains about 50 calories, so you can't eat infinite amounts. They don't really offer vitamins or minerals either. And the leading ingredient is sugar.

ALSO GOOD: Chocolate pudding pops

One pop (made by Jell-O) is only 79 calories, with 2 grams fat.

SPECIAL MENTION: Chocolate-flavored low-fat yogurt

Would you believe chocolate-raspberry yogurt? Chocolate-cherry? Chocolate-cappuccino? They're really, really chocolatey and contain only 200 calories for ¾ cup, with just 2 grams fat. They're put out by Whitney's of New York and are available in some parts of the country.

Seafood Entrées

GOOD: Haddock

Just 112 calories and 1 gram of fat for every 3½ ounces (8 percent of calories from fat).

BEST: Lobster

The winner and still champion. Steamed or boiled, it gets just 5 percent of calories from fat. You get 98 calories and less than a gram of fat in 3½ ounces. You'll need to skip the melted butter, however—try cocktail sauce instead.

BEWARE: Tuna salad

Sorry, Charlie. A cup of tuna salad, with regular mayo, provides 380 calories and 19 grams fat (45 percent of calories).

Munchies

GOOD: Baked Bugles

Unlike the regular Bugles product (with 150 calories and 8 grams of fat per serving), the kind marked "Oven Baked" are relatively low calorie (90 calories for 42 Bugles) and low-fat (2 grams fat). But like the regular product, they taste oily and crunchy. (The sodium is pretty high, though, at 300 milligrams per serving, and they don't offer many nutrients.)

BETTER: Air-popped popcorn

Three cups contain only 93 calories and a gram of fat, plus about 3 grams of dietary fiber.

BETTER YET: Fat-free baked potato chips or tortilla chips

Guiltless Gourmet No-Oil Tortilla Chips contain 110 calories for 22 chips, a respectable 4 grams fiber and zero fat. Similarly, Louise's Fat-Free Potato Chips contain about 100 calories per ounce and no fat.

Beef

GOOD: Healthy Choice Extra-Lean Low-Fat Ground Beef

Four ounces (uncooked) has 4 grams of fat—that's about 28 percent of its calories. By comparison, four ounces of regular ground beef contains 30 grams fat (77 percent of calories).

BETTER: Select-grade top and eye round

With about 20 to 25 percent of calories from fat, they're a cut above all other supermarket-grade cuts.

BEST: New brands of beef that are raised to be low in fat through diet

There are several, including Dakota Lean Meats. Most of the Dakota cuts—ranging from top sirloin to tenderloin to sirloin tips—average about 2.7 grams of fat and 130 calories for every four-ounce serving. That's a respectable 18 percent of calories from fat.

Fun Snacks and Nibbles

SMART CHOICES FOR PARTIES AND BETWEEN MEALS

mericans love to snack, whether it's at a coffee break, after school, at parties or before bedtime. In the 1980s, many of us replaced breakfast, lunch and dinner with more relaxed all-day light eating or snacking and coined a new name for it: "grazing." But traditional party and snack foods are also traditionally high in fat, calories and sodium. Today's grazing requires a healthful, well-balanced "pasture" to browse through. In this chapter, you'll find creative, low-fat appetizers and finger foods to build an elegant party menu, as well as snacks for lunches, outings and casual get-togethers. And all of them will fit into your healthy eating—and easy living—plans.

PER SERVING

115 calories

4.2 g. fat
(29% of calories)

2.3 g. dietary fiber

0 mg. fiber

207 mg. sodium

PREPARATION TIME
15 minutes

COOKING TIME
12 minutes

Caponata

serves 4

Serve this eggplant mixture on bruschetta or lettuce leaves. You can easily make this ahead—and, in fact, the flavor actually improves if you let it stand at least 2 hours.

1	teaspoon olive oil
1	eggplant, peeled and cut into 1" cubes
1	cup chopped tomatoes
1	sweet red pepper, coarsely chopped
1	green pepper, coarsely chopped
1	onion, coarsely chopped
3	cloves garlic, minced
15	black olives, pitted and chopped
1/4	cup drained capers
1/4	cup chopped fresh parsley
2	tablespoons chopped fresh marjoram
1	tablespoon red wine vinegar

Warm the oil in a large no-stick frying pan over medium-high heat. Add the eggplant and sauté for 2 minutes. Add the tomatoes, red peppers, green peppers, onions and garlic. Reduce the heat and simmer for 10 minutes, stirring occasionally. Stir in the olives, capers, parsley, marjoram and vinegar.

Bruschetta recipe on page 32

PREPARATION TIME
5 minutes

BAKING TIME
5 minutes

Photo on page 31

Bruschetta

makes 4

Bruschetta are simple garlic toasts that can be served unadorned or with fresh toppings.

> 4 slices Italian or sourdough bread
>
> 2 cloves garlic, halved lengthwise
>
> 1 tablespoon olive oil

Place the bread on a baking sheet and broil about 5" from the heat until lightly toasted on both sides. While still hot, rub one side of each slice with the garlic, pressing the juice into the toast. Using a brush, spread the oil over the garlic side of the toast.

VARIATIONS

Tomato and Watercress Bruschetta

Layer 4 bruschetta with 1 cup watercress leaves and tomato slices. Sprinkle with ¼ cup chopped red onions, 1 tablespoon drained capers and 1 teaspoon olive oil.

PER SERVING: 143 calories, 4.6 g. fat (30% of calories), 1.6 g. dietary fiber, 0 mg. fiber, 190 mg. sodium

Cucumber, Sun-Dried Tomato and Olive Bruschetta

Layer 4 bruschetta with 1 small cucumber (peeled, seeded and thinly sliced). Top with sun-dried tomato halves (soaked in hot water, drained and chopped). Sprinkle with 2 tablespoons chopped black olives and 2 tablespoons chopped fresh basil.

PER SERVING: 142 calories, 4.2 g. fat (26% of calories), 1.9 g. dietary fiber, 0 mg. fiber, 177 mg. sodium

Light 'n' Lean Nachos

serves 8

Nachos are a perennial favorite, but they're generally loaded with fat, sodium and calories. In this healthier version, potatoes replace the traditional deep-fried tortilla chips.

PER SERVING

146 calories

3.2 g. fat
(18% of calories)

2.4 g. dietary fiber

7 mg. fiber

215 mg. sodium

PREPARATION TIME
10 minutes

COOKING TIME
15 minutes

1½	pounds large potatoes, scrubbed and sliced crosswise ⅜" thick
½	cup defatted chicken broth
1⅓	cups salsa
1	cup rinsed and drained canned pinto or white beans
½	teaspoon hot-pepper sauce
⅔	cup shredded reduced-fat Monterey Jack cheese

In a 4-cup glass measuring cup, combine half of the potatoes and ¼ cup of the broth. Cover with vented plastic wrap and microwave on high power for 5 to 7 minutes, or until the potatoes are just tender.

Let stand for 5 minutes, or until cool enough to handle. Drain the potatoes and pat them dry with paper towels. Spread on a large microwave-safe serving plate.

In a small bowl, mix the salsa, beans and hot-pepper sauce. Spoon half of the mixture over the potatoes. Sprinkle with ⅓ cup of the Monterey Jack. Loosely cover with wax paper.

Microwave on medium (50% power) for 2 minutes, or until the cheese has melted. Serve immediately.

Repeat with the remaining potatoes, broth, salsa mixture and Monterey Jack.

Chef's Notes

Microwaving cheese on medium power prevents it from turning rubbery.

If you don't have a microwave, steam the potato slices until tender, about 10 minutes. Then spread them on ovenproof platters and top with the salsa mixture and cheese. Bake at 350° for 15 minutes.

Fun Snacks and Nibbles

Spinach Dip

serves 8

This dip is particularly easy. But do allow at least 30 minutes for the yogurt to drain so the dip will be nice and thick. If you're not fond of lots of garlic, use only one or two cloves. Serve with crisp fresh vegetables.

PER SERVING

57 calories

1.9 g. fat
(30% of calories)

0.6 g. dietary fiber

0.3 mg. fiber

63 mg. sodium

PREPARATION TIME
5 minutes
plus 30 minutes
draining time

COOKING TIME
5 minutes

2	cups fat-free plain yogurt
1	tablespoon olive oil
4	cloves garlic, minced
1	cup packed fresh spinach, finely chopped
$\frac{1}{4}$	teaspoon lemon juice
$\frac{1}{8}$	teaspoon ground black pepper

Spoon the yogurt into a yogurt cheese funnel or a sieve lined with cheesecloth. Place over a bowl and allow to drain for 30 minutes.

Warm the oil in a large no-stick frying pan over medium heat. Add the garlic and cook, stirring constantly, for 1 minute. Add the spinach. Cook, stirring, for 2 minutes, or until wilted. Remove from the heat.

Stir in the yogurt, lemon juice and pepper. Transfer to a shallow serving dish.

PREPARATION TIME
10 minutes

BAKING TIME
10 minutes

Photo on page 59

Fresh Tomato Salsa
with Homemade Tortilla Chips

serves 8

Goat cheese gives this traditional salsa an unexpected flavor twist. Enjoy it with these easy-to-make tortilla chips.

1	cup chopped plum tomatoes
½	cup chopped scallions
½	cup chopped fresh coriander
1	tablespoon grated lime rind
1	tablespoon lime juice
1	teaspoon olive oil
½	jalapeño pepper, seeded and minced (wear plastic gloves when handling)
1	tablespoon crumbled goat cheese
4	large flour tortillas

In a medium bowl, mix the tomatoes, scallions, coriander, lime rind, lime juice, oil and peppers. Sprinkle with the goat cheese.

Cut each tortilla into 8 wedges. Coat a large baking sheet with no-stick spray. Place the wedges on the sheet. Bake at 350° for 10 minutes, or until golden and crispy. Serve with the salsa.

Chef's Note

Plum tomatoes are small and meaty with less juice and fewer seeds than regular tomatoes. They're often called Italian tomatoes or Roma tomatoes.

Potato Chips

serves 4

It's easy to make your own healthy chips. For nice thin ones, use a manual slicing machine (inexpensive plastic ones are available at cooking stores). For a gourmet touch, try blue or purple potatoes.

2	Idaho potatoes
2	sweet potatoes

Slice the potatoes as thin as possible (about 20 slices per potato). Place 10 slices at a time on a microwave-safe rack and microwave on high power for 4 minutes, or until golden and crispy.

Watch the first batch carefully; microwaving time depends on the moisture content of the potatoes. If after 4 minutes the potatoes are not crisp, continue microwaving for 30 seconds at a time. Repeat to cook all the slices.

Chef's Note

If you don't have a microwave, place a wire rack on a baking sheet. Arrange the potato slices on the rack. Bake at 450° for 15 to 20 minutes.

PER SERVING
66 calories
0.1 g. fat (1% of calories)
1.8 g. dietary fiber
0 mg. fiber
5 mg. sodium

PREPARATION TIME
5 minutes

COOKING TIME
40 minutes

PER 2
TABLESPOONS

29 calories

0.7 g. fat
(20% of calories)

0.8 g. dietary fiber

0 mg. fiber

139 mg. sodium

PREPARATION TIME
10 minutes

Seven-Layer Skinny Dip

serves 20

Seven-layer dip always makes a big hit at parties, and this low-fat version will be equally popular. Serve it with homemade tortilla chips for "scooping."

1	can fat-free refried beans
1	cup fat-free sour cream
1/2	cup fat-free mayonnaise
1	teaspoon chili powder
1	teaspoon ground cumin
1	cup shredded fat-free Cheddar cheese
1/2	cup chopped scallions
1/2	cup sliced black olives
1	tomato, chopped
1/2	avocado, chopped

Spread the refried beans over the bottom of a 9" pie plate. In a small bowl, mix the sour cream, mayonnaise, chili powder and cumin. Spread over the beans. Sprinkle with the Cheddar, scallions, olives, tomatoes and avocados.

Chef's Note

For easy homemade fat-free refried beans, rinse and drain your favorite canned beans and mash them with a fork or in a food processor.

Fresh Tomato Salsa with Homemade Tortilla Chips recipe on page 36

PREPARATION TIME
10 minutes

Lime Dip
with Fresh Fruit

serves 4

Fresh fruit makes a lovely appetizer. In this recipe, it's served with a creamy sweet-tart dressing that's fat-free. You may substitute other fruit according to what's in season.

¼ cup fat-free mayonnaise

¼ cup fat-free sour cream

Grated rind of 1 lime

3 tablespoons lime juice

2 tablespoons honey

1 bunch red grapes

2 oranges, cut into wedges

In a small bowl, whisk together the mayonnaise, sour cream, lime rind, lime juice and honey. Place in the center of a platter and surround with the grapes and oranges.

PREPARATION TIME
15 minutes

BAKING TIME
40 minutes

Cocktail Meatballs Florentine

serves 8

Spinach and cheese are what make these versatile and delicious meatballs "florentine." Serve with warmed marinara sauce or salsa for additional flavor.

8	cloves garlic, unpeeled
1	teaspoon olive oil
4	shallots
1	cup fresh spinach leaves
1/2	cup fat-free ricotta cheese
1	egg white
2	teaspoons dried oregano
1/2	teaspoon ground black pepper
1/2	teaspoon dried dill
1/4	teaspoon ground nutmeg
12	ounces extra-lean ground beef
1/3	cup fresh whole-wheat bread crumbs

Combine the garlic and oil in a custard cup, cover with aluminum foil and bake at 400° for 15 minutes, or until soft when tested with the tip of a knife. Do not allow the garlic to brown. Let cool slightly, then slip off the skins and trim off the hard stem ends.

In a food processor, puree the garlic, shallots, spinach, ricotta and egg white. Add the oregano, pepper, dill and nutmeg.

In a large bowl, combine the beef and bread crumbs. Add the spinach mixture and mix well.

Shape into 32 meatballs. Line a jelly-roll pan with aluminum foil. Place a wire rack on the foil. Coat the rack with no-stick spray. Place the meatballs on the rack and bake at 400° for 20 to 25 minutes, or until brown.

Pita Party Pizza

makes 16 slices

Pita rounds make perfect instant pizza crusts. The feta cheese, spinach and olives give this pizza Greek flair.

PER SLICE

32 calories

0.7 g. fat
(19% of calories)

0.8 g. dietary fiber

1 mg. fiber

52 mg. sodium

2	whole-wheat pita breads
1	box (10 ounces) frozen chopped spinach, thawed and squeezed dry
$1/2$	cup shredded fat-free mozzarella cheese
$1/4$	cup crumbled feta cheese
$1/4$	cup sliced black olives
1	tomato, chopped
$1/4$	cup thinly sliced red onions

PREPARATION TIME
10 minutes

BAKING TIME
10 minutes

Prick the pitas several times with a fork. Spread the spinach over the pitas. Sprinkle with the mozzarella, feta, olives, tomatoes and onions. Place the pitas on a baking sheet and bake at 400° for 10 minutes.

To serve, cut each pizza into 8 slices.

PREPARATION TIME
5 minutes
plus chilling time

COOKING TIME
10 minutes

Festive Kabobs

makes 8

Your guests will relish these colorful tortellini skewers.

16	cheese-filled spinach tortellini
8	cheese-filled white tortellini
²/₃	cup fat-free Italian dressing
¼	cup water
16	cherry tomatoes
8	small mushrooms
16	pieces (1" × 1") yellow peppers
16	pieces (1" × 1") sweet red peppers
8	pieces (1" × 1") green peppers
¼	teaspoon olive oil

Cook the tortellini in a large pot of boiling water according to the package directions. Drain and place in a large shallow baking dish.

In a small bowl, whisk together the dressing and water. Pour over the tortellini. Add the tomatoes and mushrooms. Stir to coat.

In a 1-quart microwave-safe casserole, mix the yellow peppers, red peppers, green peppers and oil. Cover with vented plastic wrap and microwave on high power for 2 to 4 minutes, or until the peppers are crisp-tender. Add to the baking dish. Toss gently. Chill.

Evenly divide the ingredients among 8 wooden skewers.

chapter 4

Soups and Salads

OLD FAVORITES . . . AND LOTS MORE

Each region of America boasts an incredible variety of fruits, vegetables, meat, poultry and seafood that have been adopted and adapted by the immigrants who settled this country. In the East, they dreamed up new ways to use clams and oysters; in the North, they turned to the Ojibwa for wild rice. The South melded the sweet and spicy flavors of the Caribbean with European dishes; in the West, they capitalized on a garden of fresh fruits and vegetables. And in the Southwest, they adopted fiery chili peppers to season dishes of all types. The soups and salads in this chapter make the most of regional ingredients and reflect America's ethnic diversity.

Miami Black Bean Soup

serves 4

PER SERVING

244 calories

3.6 g. fat
(11% of calories)

14.6 g. dietary fiber

0 mg. cholesterol

960 mg. sodium

PREPARATION TIME
10 minutes

COOKING TIME
25 minutes

This thick, spicy soup reflects its Caribbean heritage with cumin, red-pepper flakes and jalapeño peppers.

1½	cups diced onions
2	stalks celery, diced
2	carrots, diced
4	cloves garlic, minced
1	teaspoon olive oil
3	cans (15 ounces each) black beans, rinsed and drained
2½	cups defatted chicken broth
2	cups canned crushed tomatoes
1½	tablespoons lime juice
1½	teaspoons ground cumin
½	teaspoon red-pepper flakes
⅓	cup fat-free sour cream
⅓	cup diced sweet red, yellow or green peppers
2	tablespoons sliced jalapeño peppers (wear plastic gloves when handling)

In a large saucepan over medium heat, sauté the onions, celery, carrots and garlic in the oil for 3 to 4 minutes, or until the vegetables begin to soften. Add the beans, broth, tomatoes, lime juice, cumin and red-pepper flakes. Cover and bring to a boil. Reduce the heat and simmer for 15 to 20 minutes, or until the vegetables are tender.

Serve garnished with the sour cream, sweet peppers and jalapeño peppers.

Minestrone

serves 4

In Italy, minestrone ("big soup") means just about any kind of soup made with pasta, beans and whatever vegetables are growing in the garden. In winter, it's made with canned tomatoes and root vegetables. As with most soups, reheating heightens the flavors. This recipe is easily doubled so you can have extra to freeze.

PER SERVING

240 calories

3.4 g. fat
(12% of calories)

9.4 g. dietary fiber

0 mg. cholesterol

609 mg. sodium

PREPARATION TIME
15 minutes

COOKING TIME
35 minutes

1	cup chopped onions
1	clove garlic, minced
½	teaspoon olive oil
2	cups shredded cabbage
1	cup sliced carrots
1	cup chopped spinach
½	cup sliced celery
½	cup chopped fresh parsley
2	bay leaves
2	teaspoons chopped fresh rosemary
1	teaspoon chopped fresh sage
2	cups defatted chicken broth
2	cups water
1	can (15 ounces) no-salt-added stewed tomatoes, chopped (with juice)
1	can (16 ounces) chick-peas, rinsed and drained
4	ounces spaghetti, broken in half
	Salt and ground black pepper

In a large soup pot over medium-high heat, sauté the onions and garlic in the oil for 1 minute. Add the cabbage, carrots, spinach, celery, parsley, bay leaves, rosemary and sage; sauté for 3 minutes, or until the vegetables begin to wilt. Add the broth, water, tomatoes (with juice), chick-peas and spaghetti. Cover and bring to a boil. Reduce the heat and simmer for 20 minutes. Uncover and cook for 10 minutes. Remove and discard the bay leaves. Add salt and pepper to taste.

Chef's Note
For a thinner soup, add up to 4 cups broth.

Soups and Salads

Hot and Hearty Chowder

serves 4

This hearty New England soup should hit the spot on really cold evenings. Serve with a tossed salad and cornbread for a complete meal.

PER SERVING

252 calories

4.1 g. fat
(15% of calories)

2.5 g. dietary fiber

50 mg. cholesterol

215 mg. sodium

PREPARATION TIME
10 minutes

COOKING TIME
25 minutes

12	shucked chowder clams
5	cups defatted chicken broth
2	large baking potatoes, peeled and diced
1	large onion, diced
1	stalk celery, diced
1	tablespoon minced fresh parsley
1	bay leaf
1/2	teaspoon dried oregano
1/4	teaspoon dried tarragon
1/4	teaspoon ground black pepper
8	ounces cod, cut into 1" pieces
1	cup 1% low-fat milk
1/4	teaspoon black peppercorns

In a large soup pot over medium heat, bring the clams and 2 cups of the broth to a boil. Reduce the heat to medium and simmer for 3 minutes. Remove the clams with a slotted spoon and set aside.

Add the potatoes, onions, celery, parsley, bay leaf, oregano, tarragon, ground pepper and the remaining 3 cups broth to the pot. Bring to a boil. Reduce the heat and simmer for 15 minutes, or until the vegetables are softened. Remove and discard the bay leaf.

Ladle half of the vegetables and 1 cup of the liquid into a blender. Blend until smooth. Return to the pan. Add the cod and simmer for 5 minutes, or until the cod is cooked through.

Chop the clams finely and add to the pan. Stir in the milk and heat briefly. Sprinkle with the peppercorns.

PER SERVING

99 calories

4.1 g. fat
(34% of calories)

3.5 g. dietary fiber

0 mg. cholesterol

19 mg. sodium

PREPARATION TIME
10 minutes

COOKING TIME
25 minutes

Backyard Garden Tomato Soup

serves 4

*Homegrown tomatoes capture the essence of summer in this ripe-red soup.
Use the bounty of your own garden or visit a nearby farmers' market for the
freshest ingredients. If you hanker after that just-from-the-garden flavor
during the winter, canned tomatoes give better flavor than fresh.*

1½	cups diced onions
1	sweet red pepper, diced
2	cloves garlic, minced
1	tablespoon olive oil
4	cups chopped plum tomatoes
2	cups water
¼	cup minced fresh basil
2	tablespoons minced fresh mint

In a large saucepan over medium-high heat, sauté the onions, peppers and
garlic in the oil for 1 minute. Cover, reduce the heat to low and cook for 5
minutes.

Add the tomatoes, water, basil and mint. Bring to a boil over medium heat,
then reduce the heat and simmer for 15 minutes, or until the vegetables are
just tender.

Chef's Note

Mint and tomatoes make a beautiful pair. The sweetness of mint counteracts
the natural acidity in tomatoes and eliminates the need for added sugar.

American Harvest Loaf recipe on page

PREPARATION TIME
10 minutes

COOKING TIME
25 minutes

Vibrant Chicken and Rice Soup

serves 6

Who doesn't love chicken and rice soup? This variation has a California flavor, featuring avocado, coriander and lime juice as accents.

4	cups water
2	cups defatted chicken broth
1	onion, diced
3	carrots, thinly sliced
3	boneless, skinless chicken breast halves, cubed
2½	cups cooked rice
1	small avocado, cubed
2	tomatoes, cubed
3	tablespoons minced fresh coriander
3	tablespoons lime juice
⅛	teaspoon ground red pepper
4	ounces farmer's cheese, crumbled

In a large soup pot over medium heat, bring the water, broth, onions and carrots to a boil. Reduce the heat and simmer for 10 minutes. Add the chicken and simmer for 10 minutes, or until the chicken is cooked through and the carrots are tender.

Stir in the rice, avocados, tomatoes, coriander, lime juice and pepper. Heat through but don't boil. Serve sprinkled with the farmer's cheese.

Italian Barley Soup

serves 4

Warming and hearty, this soup is typical of Italian home cooking—comforting, effortless and full of good things. It is reliable and sure to please. Serve it with lots of crusty bread and call it a meal.

1/2	cup chopped onions
1	teaspoon olive oil
1	ounce prosciutto, diced
1	tablespoon chopped fresh rosemary
1	tablespoon chopped fresh parsley
4	cups defatted chicken broth
1	medium potato, peeled and diced
2	small carrots, diced
1/2	cup quick-cooking barley
2	teaspoons grated Parmesan cheese

PREPARATION TIME
10 minutes

COOKING TIME
20 minutes

In a large saucepan over medium-high heat, sauté the onions in the oil for 3 minutes. Stir in the prosciutto, rosemary and parsley. Cook for 1 minute.

Add the broth, potatoes, carrots and barley. Bring to a boil. Reduce the heat and simmer for 10 to 15 minutes, or until the potatoes are tender. Serve sprinkled with the Parmesan.

Cobb Salad

serves 4

Cobb salads are as lovely to look at as they are to eat. For maximum effect, arrange the ingredients spoke-fashion on a bed of different varieties of lettuce.

PREPARATION TIME
15 minutes

¼	cup extra-virgin olive oil
3	tablespoons white wine vinegar
½	teaspoon minced garlic
½	teaspoon Worcestershire sauce
2	tablespoons thinly sliced basil leaves
4	cups torn mixed lettuce
8	ounces smoked turkey, cut into strips
2	hard-cooked eggs, chopped
½	small red onion, chopped
1	sweet red pepper, chopped
1	yellow pepper, chopped
2	ounces blue cheese, crumbled
⅓	cup diced turkey bacon, cooked until crisp

In a small bowl, whisk together the oil, vinegar, garlic, Worcestershire sauce and basil.

Line a large serving plate with the lettuce. Arrange the turkey, eggs, onions, red peppers and yellow peppers over the lettuce. Sprinkle with the blue cheese and bacon. Drizzle with the dressing.

Tabbouleh

serves 4

Bulgur is a very fast-cooking grain that's the mainstay of many Middle Eastern salads, including tabbouleh. If you've got red or yellow cherry tomatoes, use them in place of the chopped tomatoes for a prettier presentation.

<table>
<tr><td>1</td><td>cup defatted chicken broth</td></tr>
<tr><td>1</td><td>cup bulgur</td></tr>
<tr><td>2</td><td>cups diced tomatoes</td></tr>
<tr><td>1/2</td><td>cup chopped fresh parsley</td></tr>
<tr><td>1/4</td><td>cup chopped chives</td></tr>
<tr><td>2</td><td>tablespoons chopped fresh mint</td></tr>
<tr><td>3</td><td>tablespoons lemon juice</td></tr>
<tr><td>1 1/2</td><td>tablespoons extra-virgin olive oil</td></tr>
<tr><td>1</td><td>clove garlic, minced</td></tr>
</table>

Bring the broth to a boil in a 1-quart saucepan over high heat. Stir in the bulgur. Cover, remove from the heat and let stand for 15 minutes, or until the bulgur is tender and the liquid has been absorbed. Fluff with a fork and transfer to a large bowl.

Add the tomatoes, parsley, chives and mint. Toss lightly.

In a cup, whisk together the lemon juice, oil and garlic. Pour over the bulgur mixture and toss to mix well.

PER SERVING

222 calories

5.8 g. fat
(24% of calories)

8.5 g. dietary fiber

0 mg. cholesterol

17 mg. sodium

PREPARATION TIME
25 minutes

Southwest Three Bean Salad

serves 4

PER SERVING

204 calories

2.3 g. fat
(9% of calories)

7.4 g. dietary fiber

0 mg. cholesterol

442 mg. sodium

An eye-catching red, white and black, this makes a good luncheon salad or a side dish for grilled chicken or fish, fajitas or burgers. Canned beans work fine; just rinse and drain them to remove excess sodium and packing liquid.

PREPARATION TIME
10 minutes

¼	cup defatted chicken broth
1½	tablespoons red wine vinegar
1	teaspoon extra-virgin olive oil
½	teaspoon chili powder
1	clove garlic, minced
1	cup cooked black beans
1	cup cooked kidney beans
1	cup cooked Great Northern beans
⅓	cup diced red onions
¼	cup diced sweet red peppers
¼	cup minced fresh coriander

In a large bowl, whisk together the broth, vinegar, oil, chili powder and garlic. Add the black beans, kidney beans, Great Northern beans, onions, peppers and coriander. Toss to mix well.

PREPARATION TIME
15 minutes

COOKING TIME
5 minutes

Roasted Red Pepper Pasta Salad

serves 4

Pureeing roasted red peppers makes a pretty dressing for this light pasta salad. For a heartier dish, add sautéed chicken or turkey breasts.

10	ounces angel hair pasta
4	sweet red peppers, roasted (see note)
1/4	cup white wine vinegar
3	tablespoons defatted chicken broth
2	tablespoons chopped fresh parsley
1	tablespoon lemon juice
1	tablespoon extra-virgin olive oil
1	tablespoon chopped fresh oregano
1	teaspoon grated lemon rind
	Salt and ground black pepper

Cook the angel hair in a large pot of boiling water according to the package directions. Drain and transfer to a large bowl.

In a food processor, puree the peppers, vinegar, broth, parsley, lemon juice, oil, oregano and lemon rind; add salt and pepper to taste. Pour over the angel hair and toss to coat. Serve warm or cold.

Chef's Note

To roast peppers, broil about 5" from the heat until charred on all sides. Wrap in damp paper towels and allow to stand for 5 minutes, or until cool enough to handle. Remove and discard the skin, seeds and inner membranes.

Soups and Salads

Greek Salata

serves 4

PER SERVING

92 calories

4.8 g. fat
(47% of calories)

2.7 g. dietary fiber

4 mg. cholesterol

61 mg. sodium

Feta cheese is a hallmark of Greek salads. Here, just a sprinkle of feta gives characteristic flavor without adding a lot of fat.

PREPARATION TIME
15 minutes

1	small head red leaf lettuce, torn into bite-size pieces
2	tomatoes, cut into wedges
1	large cucumber, thinly sliced
2	green peppers, sliced
1	small red onion, sliced crosswise and separated into rings
1/3	cup lemon juice
1	tablespoon extra-virgin olive oil
2	teaspoons minced fresh dill
1	clove garlic, minced
2	tablespoons crumbled feta cheese

In a large bowl, toss together the lettuce, tomatoes, cucumbers, peppers, and onions.

In a small bowl, whisk together the lemon juice, oil, dill and garlic. Pour over the tomato mixture and toss to mix well. Serve sprinkled with the feta.

PREPARATION TIME
5 minutes

Black Bean and Corn Salad

serves 4

Here's a Southwestern salad that's perfect for a summer luncheon. To give it more zip, add hot-pepper sauce to taste.

- 1 cup cooked corn
- 2 cans (16 ounces each) black beans, rinsed and drained
- 1/4 cup chopped fresh parsley
- 2 tablespoons minced red onions
- Salt and ground black pepper
- 1/4 cup balsamic vinegar
- 1 tablespoon extra-virgin olive oil
- 1 teaspoon lemon juice
- 1 teaspoon minced garlic
- 1 teaspoon honey or brown sugar
- Lettuce leaves

In a large bowl, mix the corn, beans, parsley and onions. Add salt and pepper to taste.

In a small bowl, whisk together the vinegar, oil, lemon juice, garlic, and honey or brown sugar. Pour over the bean mixture and toss well. Serve over the lettuce.

PREPARATION TIME
5 minutes

COOKING TIME
15 minutes

Sweet Potato Salad

serves 4

What a delicious way to get disease-fighting beta-carotene! Be sure to choose orange-fleshed sweet potatoes (which are sometimes called yams in supermarkets).

2	large sweet potatoes, peeled and cubed
6	medium red potatoes, cubed
1/2	cup fat-free plain yogurt
1	teaspoon chopped fresh dill
1	tablespoon reduced-fat mayonnaise
1	teaspoon honey mustard
	Salt and ground black pepper
2	tablespoons chopped fresh parsley

Steam the sweet potatoes and red potatoes for about 15 minutes, or until tender.

In a large bowl, whisk together the yogurt, dill, mayonnaise and mustard. Add the potatoes and toss well. Add salt and pepper to taste. Sprinkle with the parsley.

Plain and Fancy Poultry

CHICKEN AND TURKEY RULE THE ROOST

The poultry twins—chicken and turkey—have become the mainstay for Americans seeking a healthier diet, and with good reason. They're not only low in fat but also incredibly versatile. Chicken and turkey can be baked, roasted, broiled, grilled, poached, stir-fried and stewed. They're wonderfully suited for all our family favorites, from casseroles and pot pie to stuffed peppers and lasagna. And if that isn't enough, they adapt as well to an elegant after-the-theater dinner party as to an easygoing Saturday-night supper.

PREPARATION TIME
10 minutes

BAKING TIME
35 minutes

Roasted Chicken with Lemon and Garlic

serves 4

Great hot or cold, this lemony chicken is perfect for a picnic or a potluck supper. The lemon juice bakes into the chicken so the meat remains moist without additional fat. Leftovers (if there are any) are delicious in salad.

1	fryer chicken (3–3½ pounds)
3	lemons
5	cloves garlic
2	sprigs fresh rosemary

Using a sharp knife, butterfly the chicken by cutting it in half along the top of the breast through the bone. Open the chicken up so that it lies flat and place, cut side down, in a baking pan.

Thinly slice 2 of the lemons. Using your fingers, gently lift the skin up from the breast and work half of the lemon slices under the skin along the breast meat. Tuck the garlic and rosemary under the chicken. Lay the remaining lemon slices on top of the chicken.

Slice the remaining lemon in half. Squeeze the juice of both halves over the chicken.

Roast the chicken at 375° for 10 minutes. Reduce the heat to 350° and continue roasting for 25 minutes, or until the juices run clear when a thigh is tested with a knife. Remove the skin before serving the chicken.

Spicy Corn on the Cob recipe on page 168

Plain and Fancy Poultry

Grilled Southwestern-Style Drumsticks

serves 4

PER SERVING

204 calories

5.7 g. fat
(25% of calories)

0 g. dietary fiber

82 mg. cholesterol

376 mg. sodium

Kids will love this one! And since it's about as easy as they come, so will you. Preheat the grill while the chicken marinates.

PREPARATION TIME
5 minutes
plus 20 minutes
marinating time

COOKING TIME
20 minutes

1	tablespoon garlic powder
1	tablespoon onion powder
1	tablespoon paprika
1	tablespoon chili powder
1	teaspoon ground cumin
1/2	teaspoon salt
1	cup dark beer or apple cider
8	chicken drumsticks, skin removed

In a resealable plastic bag, combine the garlic powder, onion powder, paprika, chili powder, cumin, and salt. Shake the bag to mix. Add the beer or apple cider and drumsticks. Shake well. Refrigerate for 20 minutes or up to 24 hours, turning occasionally.

Remove the drumsticks from the bag; reserve the marinade. Place the drumsticks on a plate and lightly coat with no-stick spray.

Grill for 20 minutes, or until the juices run clear when a drumstick is tested with a knife. Baste occasionally during the first 15 minutes with the reserved marinade. Discard the remaining marinade.

PREPARATION TIME
5 minutes

COOKING TIME
20 minutes

Lemon-Herb Chicken Breasts

serves 4

Serve this lemony chicken over pasta, rice or polenta to soak up the herb-infused juices.

2	tablespoons all-purpose flour
	Salt and ground black pepper
4	boneless, skinless chicken breasts halves (4 ounces each)
1	clove garlic, minced
1/4	cup defatted chicken broth
12	thin strips lemon rind
2	tablespoons lemon juice
1	teaspoon chopped fresh oregano
1	tablespoon chopped fresh basil

Season the flour with salt and pepper to taste. Dip the chicken in the flour to coat lightly on all sides; shake off excess flour.

In a large no-stick frying pan over medium-high heat, sauté the garlic for 1 minute, or until soft. Add the chicken and sauté for 5 minutes per side, or until cooked through and no longer pink when cut with a knife. Transfer the chicken to a plate.

Add the broth, lemon rind, lemon juice, and oregano to the pan and bring to a boil. Reduce the heat and simmer for 5 minutes, or until the liquid is reduced by half. Return the chicken to the pan to warm through. Sprinkle with the basil.

Chicken Parmesan

serves 4

Breaded cutlets are an American tradition. To trim the fat from this popular recipe, we used just a smidgen of olive oil and baked the cutlets rather than pan-frying them. This dish is delicious served on a bed of hot pasta.

1	tablespoon olive oil
1	tablespoon minced garlic
$\frac{1}{2}$	teaspoon ground black pepper
2	teaspoons dried oregano
1	cup fresh bread crumbs
2	tablespoons grated Parmesan cheese
4	boneless, skinless chicken breast halves (4 ounces each)
1	cup tomato sauce, heated

In a shallow bowl, mix the oil, garlic, pepper and 1 teaspoon of the oregano. On a sheet of wax paper, mix the bread crumbs, Parmesan and the remaining 1 teaspoon oregano.

Dip the chicken into the oil mixture to coat both sides. Dip into the bread crumb mixture to coat well.

Coat a baking sheet with no-stick spray. Place the chicken on the sheet and mist with no-stick spray. Bake at 400° for 5 minutes. Turn the pieces and bake for 10 minutes, or until the chicken is crisp and golden brown.

Serve topped with the tomato sauce.

PER SERVING

158 calories

4.6 g. fat
(27% of calories)

0.7 g. dietary fiber

48 mg. cholesterol

260 mg. sodium

PREPARATION TIME
10 minutes

BAKING TIME
15 minutes

Chicken and Seafood Gumbo

serves 6

Filé powder (ground sassafras leaves) is what gives gumbo authentic Creole flavor. Look for it in the spice section of the supermarket.

PER SERVING

152 calories

4.6 g. fat
(27% of calories)

1.6 g. dietary fiber

96 mg. cholesterol

330 mg. sodium

PREPARATION TIME
10 minutes

COOKING TIME
30 minutes

1	tablespoon canola oil
1	tablespoon all-purpose flour
1½	cups diced onions
1	green pepper, diced
¼	cup diced celery
1	can (14½ ounces) no-salt-added tomatoes, chopped
1	can (10 ounces) tomatoes with chilies, chopped
1½	cups water
8	ounces boneless, skinless chicken breast, diced
8	ounces peeled and deveined shrimp
1	cup shucked oysters
½	teaspoon filé powder
2	cups hot cooked rice

In a 4-quart saucepan, mix the oil and flour. Cook, stirring constantly, over medium heat for 3 to 5 minutes, or until the mixture turns dark brown but does not burn. Add the onions, peppers and celery. Cook for 3 to 4 minutes, or until the vegetables begin to soften.

Add the tomatoes, tomatoes with chilies and water; bring to a boil. Cook for 10 minutes. Add the chicken and cook for 5 minutes. Add the shrimp, oysters and filé powder and cook for 5 minutes, or just until the seafood is cooked through. Serve with the rice.

PREPARATION TIME
10 minutes

BAKING TIME
30 minutes

Chicken and
Black Bean Lasagna

serves 4

Bake two pans of this zesty lasagna at a time—one to enjoy now, the other to freeze for later. To easily freeze lasagna, line the baking dish with foil before assembling the lasagna; freeze uncovered. When frozen, remove the lasagna from the dish, wrap in the foil and return to the freezer.

1	can (28 ounces) low-sodium tomatoes, drained and chopped
1	can (4 ounces) chopped green chili peppers, drained
1	can (8 ounces) low-sodium tomato sauce
1	can (15 ounces) black beans, rinsed and drained
1	teaspoon ground cumin
1	teaspoon chili powder
6	no-boil lasagna noodles
1½	cups fat-free ricotta cheese
2	cups chopped cooked chicken breast
2	cups shredded reduced-fat Cheddar cheese

In a medium bowl, mix the tomatoes, peppers and tomato sauce.

In a small bowl, mix the beans, cumin and chili powder. Lightly mash the beans with a fork.

Coat an 8" × 8" baking dish with no-stick spray. Spoon ½ cup of the tomato mixture into the dish.

Place 2 of the noodles over the sauce. Top with one-third of the beans, one-third of the ricotta and one-third of the chicken. Cover with ½ cup of the Cheddar and one-third of the remaining tomato sauce. Repeat twice.

Top with the remaining ½ cup Cheddar.

Bake at 375° for 30 minutes, or until bubbling.

PREPARATION TIME
10 minutes

COOKING TIME
25 minutes

Chicken Cacciatore

serves 4

Cacciatore means "hunter," and this chicken dish, made with dark-meat thighs, is reminiscent of the game dishes of the Italian countryside: fragrant stews of tomatoes, onions and herbs. Serve this over rice to absorb the sauce.

4	chicken thighs (5 ounces each)
2	cups chopped canned tomatoes, drained
1	cup chopped mushrooms
¼	cup red wine or defatted chicken broth
¼	cup chopped fresh parsley
3	cloves garlic, minced
4	black olives, pitted and chopped
2	cups hot cooked brown rice

Remove the skin and any excess fat from the chicken.

Coat a large no-stick frying pan with no-stick spray. Place over medium heat until hot. Add the chicken and brown on all sides.

Add the tomatoes, mushrooms, wine or broth, parsley and garlic. Reduce the heat and simmer for 20 minutes, or until the chicken is tender and no longer pink when tested with a knife.

Stir in the olives. Serve over the rice.

Chef's Note

Use a combination of different mushrooms for the most flavor.
Good choices include portobello, shiitake, cremini and button mushrooms.

Turkey Noodle Casserole

serves 4

PER SERVING

617 calories

12.6 g. fat
(18% of calories)

3.3 g. dietary fiber

129 mg. cholesterol

642 mg. sodium

This old-fashioned casserole has been updated and streamlined with cooked turkey and a low-fat cheese sauce. Serve with steamed broccoli and baked potatoes to round out a classic dinner.

PREPARATION TIME
20 minutes

BAKING TIME
30 minutes

4	cups sliced mushrooms
1	tablespoon water
2	teaspoons olive oil
1/3	cup minced onions
2	tablespoons white wine or apple juice
1/4	cup all-purpose flour
2	cups defatted chicken broth
1¾	cups skim milk
1/4	cup reduced-fat cream cheese
1/2	teaspoon dried thyme
10	ounces yolk-free noodles
2	cups chopped cooked turkey breast
1	cup frozen peas
1	jar (2 ounces) diced pimientos
1/3	cup grated Parmesan cheese
1/3	cup seasoned bread crumbs
1/2	teaspoon ground black pepper

In a 2-quart saucepan, mix the mushrooms, water and oil. Cook over medium-high heat, stirring frequently, for 7 minutes, or until the mushrooms brown and the pan is dry. Add the onions and wine or apple juice. Cook for 2 minutes.

Stir in the flour and cook for 3 minutes. Gradually stir in the broth, milk, cream cheese and thyme. Cook, stirring, for 5 minutes, or until the sauce has slightly thickened.

Cook the noodles in a large pot of boiling water according to the package directions. Drain well and transfer to a large bowl. Stir in the mushroom sauce, turkey, peas, pimientos and Parmesan.

Coat a 3-quart casserole with no-stick spray. Add the turkey mixture. Sprinkle with the bread crumbs and pepper. Bake at 375° for 20 to 30 minutes, or until bubbling.

Turkey Pot Pie
with Buttermilk Biscuit Crust

serves 4

Yes! You can have old-fashioned turkey pot pie in less than 45 minutes. Cooked turkey and frozen mixed vegetables help streamline this family favorite.

PER SERVING

331 calories

6.4 g. fat
(18% of calories)

3.2 g. dietary fiber

64 mg. cholesterol

536 mg. sodium

PREPARATION TIME
15 minutes

BAKING TIME
30 minutes

1	cup all-purpose flour
1	teaspoon baking powder
1/4	teaspoon baking soda
	Pinch of salt
1	tablespoon plus 2 teaspoons chilled butter, cut into small pieces
1/4	cup low-fat buttermilk
3	tablespoons reduced-fat sour cream
1 3/4	cups defatted chicken broth
1/3	cup chopped onions
2	teaspoons minced garlic
2 1/2	tablespoons cornstarch
1/4	teaspoon poultry seasoning
1/2	teaspoon dried thyme
1/4	teaspoon dried sage
2	cups frozen mixed peas, carrots and cauliflower, thawed
2	cups diced cooked turkey breast

In a medium bowl, mix the flour, baking powder, baking soda and salt. Cut in the butter with 2 knives until the mixture resembles fine crumbs. Stir in the buttermilk and sour cream to form a dough. Turn the dough onto a sheet of plastic wrap and flatten it into a large disk; wrap tightly. Refrigerate while you make the filling.

Bring 1/4 cup of the broth to a boil in a large frying pan. Add the onions and garlic. Cook for 2 minutes.

In a small bowl, mix the cornstarch, poultry seasoning, thyme, and sage. Stir in the remaining 1 1/2 cups broth until smooth. Add to the frying pan. Cook until the mixture comes to a boil and thickens. Remove from the heat and add the vegetables and turkey. Pour into an 8" × 8" baking dish.

Cut the biscuit dough into four sections; arrange on top of the filling. Bake at 425° for 30 minutes, or until the biscuits are golden brown and the filling is bubbling.

Turkey Stuffed Peppers

serves 4

Red and green peppers are the serving "boats" for well-seasoned turkey-rice stuffing in this recipe. For variety, try other colors of peppers such as yellow and purple, but remember that purple peppers turn green when cooked.

1	large sweet red pepper
1	large green pepper
1½	cups cooked brown rice
½	cup diced onions
¼	cup defatted chicken broth
1	teaspoon grated orange rind
½	teaspoon ground black pepper
6	ounces ground turkey breast
1	carrot, shredded
¼	cup diced dill pickles
1	egg white
3	cloves garlic
1	teaspoon Dijon mustard
¼	cup fat-free sour cream
½	teaspoon dried dill

Cut the peppers in half lengthwise and remove the seeds and membranes. Place in a pot of boiling water for 1 minute. Drain.

In a large no-stick frying pan, mix the rice, onions, broth, orange rind and black pepper. Cook over medium heat for 3 minutes. Add the turkey and cook, breaking up the pieces with a spoon, until the turkey is no longer pink. Remove from the heat.

Stir in the carrots, pickles, egg white, garlic and mustard.

Fill the pepper halves with the turkey mixture. Place in a shallow pan large enough to hold the pepper halves in a single layer. Pour about ½" of water into the pan and bake at 375° for 15 minutes.

In a cup, mix the sour cream and dill. Serve with the peppers.

PREPARATION TIME
15 minutes

COOKING TIME
15 minutes

Turkey Stir-Fry

serves 4

You may vary the vegetables to accommodate what's on hand. Serve the stir-fry over rice.

1	tablespoon minced fresh ginger
1	clove garlic, minced
1	tablespoon apricot preserves
1	tablespoon reduced-sodium soy sauce
1	tablespoon white vinegar
1	pound boneless, skinless turkey breast
1	large onion, thinly sliced
4	ounces snow peas
1	sweet red pepper, thinly sliced
2	teaspoons canola oil
1	tablespoon cornstarch
3/4	cup defatted chicken broth

In a large bowl, mix the ginger, garlic, preserves, soy sauce and vinegar. Cut the turkey into thin strips, add to the bowl and mix well.

In a large no-stick frying pan over medium-high heat, stir-fry the onions, snow peas and peppers in the oil for 5 minutes, or until just tender. Remove with a slotted spoon and set aside.

Add the turkey, with the marinade, to the pan. Stir-fry for 5 minutes, or until the turkey is cooked through. Return the vegetables to the pan.

In a cup, mix the cornstarch and broth until smooth. Add to the pan. Stir until thick.

chapter 6

Seafood for All Occasions

FAMILY PLEASERS PLUS COMPANY FARE

Mussels, scallops and flounder. Catfish, soft-shelled crabs and shrimp. Swordfish, salmon and orange roughy. This list just begins to touch on the incredible variety of finned and shelled creatures that inhabit our lakes, rivers and oceans—and lend versatility and flavor to our diets. Seafood and fish—often called "brain food," and for good reason—are excellent sources of a whole alphabet of vitamins and minerals from vitamin A to zinc. Many fish are virtually fat-free, and what fat they do contain is in the form of heart-healthy omega-3 fatty acids.

Teriyaki Salmon

serves 4

The flavors of the Orient inspired this simple dish. Serve with rice and cucumber salad.

1/3	cup reduced-sodium soy sauce
2	tablespoons mirin (rice wine) or apple juice
2	tablespoons chopped scallions
2	teaspoons grated fresh ginger
2	tablespoons honey
3	tablespoons lemon juice
4	salmon steaks

PREPARATION TIME
5 minutes
plus 30 minutes
marinating time

COOKING TIME
20 minutes

In a resealable plastic bag, mix the soy sauce, mirin or apple juice, scallions, ginger, honey and lemon juice. Add the salmon and shake well. Refrigerate for 30 minutes, turning occasionally.

Coat a broiler pan with no-stick spray and place the salmon on it. Transfer the marinade to a 1-quart saucepan and bring to a boil over medium-high heat. Cook, stirring occasionally, for 8 minutes, or until reduced by half.

Broil the salmon about 4" from the heat for 10 to 12 minutes, or until the fish flakes easily when tested with a fork; turn halfway through the cooking time. Serve with the reduced marinade.

PREPARATION TIME
20 minutes

BAKING TIME
15 minutes

Cornmeal-Breaded Catfish with Sweet Pepper Relish

serves 4

Available throughout the year, catfish is a mild, delicate fish that blends well with the stronger flavors of Southwestern dishes. Serve this entrée with fresh green beans and sliced tomatoes.

Sweet Pepper Relish

3/4	cup cider vinegar
2	tablespoons apple juice
2	tablespoons honey
1/2	cup diced sweet red peppers
1/2	cup diced green peppers
1/2	cup diced yellow peppers
1/3	cup thinly sliced onions
1	tablespoon chopped fresh mint

Catfish

3/4	cup low-fat buttermilk
3/4	cup cornmeal
1	tablespoon Cajun seafood seasoning
4	catfish fillets

TO MAKE THE SWEET PEPPER RELISH
In a 1-quart saucepan, mix the vinegar, apple juice and honey. Stir in the red peppers, green peppers, yellow peppers and onions. Bring to a boil over medium-high heat and cook for 1 minute, or until the onions are wilted. Stir in the mint. Remove from the heat.

TO MAKE THE CATFISH
Place the buttermilk in a shallow dish. Mix the cornmeal and Cajun seasoning on a piece of wax paper. Dip the fillets in the buttermilk and then in the cornmeal, coating each fillet thoroughly.

Line a baking sheet with aluminum foil and coat with no-stick spray. Place the fillets on the sheet and coat lightly with no-stick spray. Bake at 475° for 10 to 15 minutes, or until lightly browned and the fish flakes when tested with a fork.

Strain excess liquid from the relish and serve with the fillets.

PREPARATION TIME
10 minutes
plus 20 minutes
marinating time

COOKING TIME
10 minutes

Grilled Swordfish Kabobs

serves 4

The meaty texture of swordfish makes it ideal for grilling. Other fish that would work well in this recipe are tuna, halibut and mako shark.

1/4	cup defatted chicken broth
1	tablespoon drained green peppercorns, crushed
1	teaspoon olive oil
1	teaspoon lemon juice
1 1/4	pounds swordfish steak
1	green pepper
1	lemon
8	cherry tomatoes

In a medium bowl, mix the broth, peppercorns, oil and lemon juice. Cut the swordfish into 20 equal cubes. Add to the bowl and stir to coat. Cover and refrigerate for 20 minutes to marinate.

Cut the green pepper into 1½" pieces. Cut the lemon in half lengthwise, then crosswise into ½" slices.

Remove the fish from the marinade; reserve the marinade. Thread the peppers, swordfish, lemon slices and tomatoes onto 4 metal skewers, dividing the ingredients evenly among the skewers. Brush with the reserved marinade and grill for 6 to 10 minutes, turning once. Discard the remaining marinade.

Chesapeake Bay Crab Cakes with Red Pepper Tartar Sauce

serves 4

Maryland and the Chesapeake Bay region are renowned for their crab cakes, which are crispy on the outside and tender on the inside.

PER SERVING

247 calories

8.8 g. fat
(33% of calories)

0.4 g. dietary fiber

108 mg. cholesterol

537 mg. sodium

Crab Cakes

2	egg whites
1	tablespoon lemon juice
1/4	teaspoon dry mustard
1/4	teaspoon hot-pepper sauce
1/4	teaspoon Worcestershire sauce
1	pound crabmeat, well-drained
1/4	cup minced onions
3	tablespoons thinly sliced scallions
1/2	cup crushed oyster crackers
1/4	cup reduced-fat mayonnaise

Red Pepper Tartar Sauce

1/2	cup fat-free plain yogurt
1/4	cup minced sweet red peppers
2	tablespoons minced onions
1/8	teaspoon ground red pepper

PREPARATION TIME
10 minutes

COOKING TIME
8 minutes

TO MAKE THE CRAB CAKES

In a medium bowl, mix the egg whites, lemon juice, mustard, hot-pepper sauce and Worcestershire sauce. Add the crabmeat, onions and scallions and stir gently. Stir in the oyster crackers and mayonnaise. Form into 12 patties.

Line a baking sheet with aluminum foil and coat with no-stick spray. Place the patties on the sheet. Broil about 3" from the heat for 5 to 8 minutes, or until lightly browned, turning once.

TO MAKE THE RED PEPPER TARTAR SAUCE

In a food processor, process the yogurt, red peppers, onions and ground red pepper until smooth. Serve with the crab cakes.

Chef's Note

Drain the crabmeat thoroughly, pressing it in a sieve to remove extra liquid.

Seafood for All Occasions

Grilled Shrimp with Orzo

serves 4

PER SERVING

351 calories

3.3 g. fat
(9% of calories)

1.2 g. dietary fiber

131 mg. cholesterol

456 mg. sodium

Orzo pasta cooks very quickly, making it a good choice for weeknight meals. Here, it pairs with spicy marinated shrimp.

2	tablespoons reduced-sodium soy sauce
1	tablespoon rice vinegar
2	tablespoons honey
1	teaspoon cornstarch
2	teaspoons sesame oil
12	ounces medium shrimp, peeled and deveined
1	cup orzo
1/4	cup defatted chicken broth
1	tablespoon minced garlic
2	teaspoons chopped fresh ginger
1/4	cup sliced scallions
1/2–1	teaspoon minced jalapeño peppers (wear plastic gloves when handling)
1/2	cup shredded carrots
1/2	cup diced sweet red peppers

In a resealable plastic bag, mix the soy sauce, vinegar, honey, cornstarch, oil and shrimp. Shake well. Refrigerate for 15 minutes, turning occasionally.

Remove the shrimp, reserving the marinade. Grill the shrimp for 3 minutes, or until pink.

Cook the orzo in a pot of boiling water according to the package directions. Drain.

Bring the broth to a boil in a large no-stick frying pan over medium-high heat. Add the garlic, ginger, scallions, jalapeño peppers, carrots and red peppers. Cook for 2 to 3 minutes. Add the orzo, grilled shrimp and reserved marinade. Bring to a boil. Cook for 1 to 2 minutes, or until the sauce thickens.

PREPARATION TIME
10 minutes
plus 15 minutes
marinating time

COOKING TIME
15 minutes

PREPARATION TIME
10 minutes

COOKING TIME
7 minutes

Spicy Jumbo Shrimp

serves 4

It's the chili peppers and hot-pepper sauce that give this shrimp its piquant flavor. Serve hot with rice or oven fries. Or serve cold on a bed of lettuce.

1	pound jumbo shrimp, peeled and deveined
1	teaspoon olive oil
1/2	cup white wine or water
2	tablespoons lemon juice
1	small jalapeño pepper, finely chopped (wear plastic gloves when handling)
	Dash of hot-pepper sauce

In a large no-stick frying pan over medium-high heat, sauté the shrimp in the oil for 1 minute. Add the wine or water, lemon juice, peppers and hot-pepper sauce. Cover and cook for 3 minutes, or until the shrimp turn pink.

Using a slotted spoon, transfer the shrimp to a serving bowl. Cook the sauce over high heat for 3 minutes, or until it is slightly reduced. Pour over the shrimp. Serve warm or cold.

Provençal Tuna Loaf

serves 4

This is perfect picnic fare. A loaf of crusty bread is hollowed out and stuffed with a savory mixture of tuna and vegetables. You can prepare it ahead and keep it chilled until needed.

PER SERVING

356 calories

7.7 g. fat
(19% of calories)

1.8 g. dietary fiber

17 mg. cholesterol

552 mg. sodium

PREPARATION TIME
10 minutes
plus 15 minutes
standing time

1	small round loaf crusty Italian bread
1	tablespoon olive oil
2	tablespoons balsamic vinegar
1	garlic clove, halved
1/8	teaspoon crushed red-pepper flakes
1	teaspoon dried thyme
1	jar (7 ounces) roasted sweet red peppers, drained
1	can (7 ounces) tuna packed in water, drained
1	large tomato, thinly sliced
1/2	cup thinly sliced red onions
1	teaspoon drained capers
1	cup watercress or small lettuce leaves
	Salt and ground black pepper

Halve the bread horizontally; remove the soft crumbs from inside the top half and reserve for another use. Brush the cut sides of both halves with the oil and vinegar, then rub with the cut garlic. Sprinkle with the red-pepper flakes and thyme.

On the bottom half of the loaf, layer the red peppers, tuna, tomatoes, onions, capers and watercress or lettuce. Sprinkle with the salt and black pepper. Press the top half of the loaf over the filling; wrap tightly in plastic wrap. Let it stand at room temperature for 15 minutes for the flavors to blend; slice into wedges.

Steamed Mussels
with Tomatoes and Saffron

serves 4

Saffron complements the subtle flavor of mussels. Although saffron is expensive, you need only a small amount for big impact.

1½	cups diced onions
1	tablespoon olive oil
4	cloves garlic, minced
2	cans (14½ ounces each) no-salt-added tomatoes, drained and chopped
2	cups defatted chicken broth
½	teaspoon saffron threads, crushed
4	dozen large mussels, scrubbed and debearded

In a soup pot over medium heat, sauté the onions in the oil for 5 minutes, or until the onions begin to wilt. Add the garlic and sauté for 30 seconds. Add the tomatoes, broth and saffron. Bring to a boil. Partially cover the pot, reduce the heat and simmer for 10 minutes.

Add the mussels. Cover and cook over high heat for 10 minutes, or until the mussels open; shake the pot occasionally. Discard any mussels that have not opened. Serve the mussels in shallow bowls and spoon the tomato mixture over them.

Chef's Note

To prepare mussels for cooking, scrub them under cold running water. Discard any that are already open or have broken shells. Remove the "beard" (the clump of strong, dark material that clings to the shell) from each mussel by tugging it off with your fingers or clipping it off. Don't debeard mussels until right before cooking or they will die and spoil.

PER SERVING

214 calories

6.5 g. fat
(27% of calories)

2.4 g. dietary fiber

63 mg. cholesterol

588 mg. sodium

PREPARATION TIME
10 minutes

COOKING TIME
25 minutes

PREPARATION TIME
15 minutes

COOKING TIME
30 minutes

Seafood Creole

serves 4

New Orleans and the bayou country of Louisiana are the birthplace of Creole cooking. In this recipe, fresh shrimp and fish pair with a spicy sauce.

2	cups diced onions
1	teaspoon olive oil
1	green pepper, diced
$3/4$	cup diced celery
3	cloves garlic, minced
2	cans ($14 1/2$ ounces each) no-salt-added tomatoes, chopped
1	teaspoon dried thyme
1	bay leaf
$1/4$	teaspoon ground red pepper
8	ounces medium shrimp, peeled and deveined
8	ounces cod or orange roughy fillets, cut into 1" pieces
2	cups hot cooked rice

In a soup pot over medium-high heat, sauté the onions in the oil for 2 minutes. Add the green peppers and celery; cook for 2 minutes. Add the garlic; cook for 1 minute.

Add the tomatoes (with juice), thyme, bay leaf and red pepper. Bring to a boil. Reduce the heat to medium and simmer for 15 to 20 minutes, or until the vegetables are just tender.

Add the shrimp and fish. Cover and cook for 3 to 5 minutes, or until the shrimp turns pink and the fish is opaque.

Remove and discard the bay leaf. Serve the shrimp mixture over the rice.

Cape Cod Scallops with Tomatoes

serves 4

PER SERVING

182 calories

3 g. fat
(15% of calories)

2 g. dietary fiber

47 mg. cholesterol

256 mg. sodium

This dish has the consistency of a chunky stew. Serve it over rice or pasta.

2	cups sliced mushrooms
1	cup sliced onions
1	teaspoon olive oil
1½	cups diced tomatoes
1	cup defatted chicken broth
1¼	pounds sea scallops
3	tablespoons minced fresh parsley
2	tablespoons lemon juice
½	teaspoon dried basil
¼	teaspoon dried rosemary
1	clove garlic, minced

PREPARATION TIME
10 minutes

COOKING TIME
20 minutes

In a large no-stick frying pan over medium-high heat, sauté the mushrooms and onions in the oil for 5 minutes. Add the tomatoes and broth. Bring to a boil.

Add the scallops, parsley, lemon juice, basil, rosemary and garlic. Reduce the heat and simmer for 5 minutes, or until the scallops are opaque. Using a slotted spoon, transfer the scallops and vegetables to a serving bowl.

Raise the heat to high and boil the stock for 5 minutes, or until reduced by half. Pour over the scallop mixture.

Bouillabaisse

serves 4

Bouillabaisse is a traditional French stew brimming with seafood. It's ideal for wintry evenings, served in crockery bowls with crunchy toast and a tossed salad.

PER SERVING

420 calories

7.9 g. fat
(17% of calories)

3.4 g. dietary fiber

148 mg. cholesterol

474 mg. sodium

PREPARATION TIME
10 minutes

COOKING TIME
20 minutes

1	tablespoon olive oil
2	bottles (8 ounces each) clam juice
1	cup chopped onions
2	leeks, thinly sliced
5	cloves garlic, minced
12	ounces small red potatoes, quartered
1	can (28 ounces) chopped Italian plum tomatoes (with juice)
1	pound halibut, cut into 2" cubes
8	ounces bay scallops
8	ounces large shrimp, peeled and deveined
2–3	tablespoons chopped fresh tarragon or basil
	Salt and ground black pepper

In a soup pot over medium-high heat, bring the oil and ¼ cup of the clam juice to a boil. Add the onions, leeks, garlic and potatoes. Cook for 3 to 5 minutes, or until the onions are lightly browned. Add the tomatoes (with juice); bring to a boil. Cook for 10 minutes.

Add the halibut, scallops and shrimp. Cook for 5 minutes, or until the fish is opaque and flakes easily when tested with a fork. Stir in the tarragon or basil. Add salt and pepper to taste.

PER SERVING

153 calories

1.5 g. fat
(9% of calories)

1.8 g. dietary fiber

56 mg. cholesterol

183 mg. sodium

PREPARATION TIME
10 minutes

BAKING TIME
15 minutes

Stuffed Flounder Florentine

serves 4

Flounder is prized for its fine texture and delicate flavor. It is sometimes mislabeled as sole, but only Dover sole is the real thing—the rest is actually flounder.

1	box (10 ounces) frozen chopped spinach, thawed and squeezed dry
1/2	cup fat-free ricotta cheese
1/4	cup dry bread crumbs
2	tablespoons fat-free sour cream
2	tablespoons chopped onions
1/4	teaspoon ground nutmeg
	Dash of hot-pepper sauce
	Salt and ground black pepper
4	flounder fillets
2	tablespoons orange juice

In a medium bowl, mix the spinach, ricotta, bread crumbs, sour cream, onions, nutmeg and hot-pepper sauce. Add salt and pepper to taste.

Spread the spinach mixture over the fillets to about 1/2" from the edge. Starting at the thin end, roll up the fillets. Secure with toothpicks.

Coat an 11" × 7" baking dish with no-stick spray. Place the fillets in the dish and drizzle with the orange juice.

Bake at 350° for 15 minutes, or until the fish is opaque and flakes when tested with a fork.

chapter 7

Meaty Entrées

BEEF, PORK AND LAMB RECIPES THAT CAN'T MISS

The heartland of America raises some of the best beef, pork and lamb in the world. But it's far different from the meat that our grandparents remember. Producers heard the consumer speak, and the consumer said, "I want less fat in my meat." So today's cuts are lean and meaty but just as versatile as ever. There are even new cuts that are especially lean but also tender. So don't feel guilty about enjoying meat. Eat it often in low-fat versions of favorites like steak sandwiches, beef stew, pork and sauerkraut, pork barbecue and lamb chops.

PREPARATION TIME
10 minutes

COOKING TIME
1¾ hours

Old-Fashioned Pot Roast

serves 6

Here's a slimmed-down version of an all-American favorite. Leftovers are great for sandwiches and super-quick dinners.

1	beef top round roast (1½ pounds), trimmed of all visible fat
1	cup tomato juice
½	cup red wine or defatted beef broth
1	tablespoon Dijon mustard
1	teaspoon dried rosemary
1	pound baby carrots
12	ounces new red potatoes, peeled
8	small onions
3	stalks celery, sliced into 1" pieces

Lightly coat a Dutch oven with no-stick spray. Add the beef and brown on all sides over medium-high heat. Transfer the beef to a plate. Add the tomato juice, wine or broth, mustard and rosemary to the pot. Mix well and bring to a boil over high heat. Return the beef to the pot.

Cover and bake at 325° for 45 minutes. Add the carrots, potatoes, onions and celery. Cover and bake for 45 to 60 minutes, or until the beef is tender.

PREPARATION TIME
10 minutes

COOKING TIME
15 minutes

Philadelphia Steak Sandwiches

serves 4

Rocky Balboa, the boxer-hero of the movies, introduced millions of Americans to Philadelphia's beloved steak sandwich. This low-fat version features reduced-fat mozzarella and plenty of sautéed vegetables. If you're adventuresome, add zing with hot cherry peppers.

1	sweet red pepper, diced
1	green pepper, diced
1	medium onion, diced
8	mushrooms, thinly sliced
2	tablespoons sliced garlic
12	ounces beef round tip steak, sliced paper thin (see note)
1/4	cup ketchup
1	teaspoon dried oregano
1/4	teaspoon ground black pepper
1	cup shredded reduced-fat mozzarella cheese
4	steak rolls, split and warmed

Coat a large no-stick frying pan with no-stick spray and warm over medium-high heat for 2 minutes. Add the sweet red peppers, green peppers, onions and mushrooms. Sauté for 5 minutes, or until browned.

Add the garlic and steak. Sauté for 3 minutes, or until the steak is no longer pink. Stir in the ketchup, oregano and black pepper. Sprinkle with the mozzarella. Cover and cook over low heat for 5 minutes, or until the mozzarella melts. Divide among the rolls.

Chef's Note
Freezing the steak for about 20 minutes will firm it enough to make thin-slicing easier.

Spicy Beef Burgers

Serves 4

Nothing could be faster or easier for summer weeknight dinners.

1   pound extra-lean ground round

2   tablespoons barbecue sauce

1   tablespoon steak sauce

1   tablespoon minced garlic

1   tablespoon chopped jalapeño peppers
     (wear plastic gloves when handling)

1   teaspoon chili powder

4   hamburger buns, split

1   tablespoon fat-free mayonnaise

In a medium bowl, mix the beef, barbecue sauce, steak sauce, garlic, peppers and chili powder. Form into 4 patties. Grill for 4 minutes per side, or until cooked through.

Toast the buns, spread with the mayonnaise and top with the patties.

PREPARATION TIME
5 minutes

COOKING TIME
8 minutes

PREPARATION TIME
15 minutes

COOKING TIME
10 minutes

Texas Beef Soft Tacos

Serves 4

By using soft flour tortillas instead of fried corn shells, we cut fat on this Tex-Mex favorite.

12	ounces beef tenderloin, trimmed of all visible fat
1½	teaspoons ground cumin
¼	cup defatted chicken broth
1	cup chopped sweet red peppers
3	cloves garlic, minced
2	canned chipotle chili peppers in adobo sauce, minced
½	cup mild salsa
8	large flour tortillas
3	ounces shredded reduced-fat Monterey Jack cheese
¼	cup fat-free sour cream
¼	cup chopped fresh cilantro

Cut the beef across the grain into very thin strips. Place in a large bowl, sprinkle with the cumin and toss well.

Bring the broth to a boil in a large no-stick frying pan over medium-high heat. Add the red peppers and garlic; cook for 3 minutes. Transfer to a plate. Add the beef to the pan and cook for 5 minutes. Stir in the chili peppers, salsa and the red pepper mixture. Cook for 2 minutes.

Wrap the tortillas in plastic wrap and microwave on high power for 1 minute. Divide the beef mixture among the tortillas, top with the Monterey Jack, sour cream and cilantro. Roll up.

Meaty Entrées

Grilled Marinated Flank Steak

Serves 4

Flank steak is very lean, yet it's often overlooked because it can be tough. This recipe keeps it moist and tender by marinating it and then cooking it very quickly on the grill.

1	pound flank steak
1/4	cup lemon juice
1/4	cup reduced-sodium soy sauce
1	teaspoon minced garlic
1	teaspoon grated fresh ginger
1	teaspoon chopped jalapeño peppers (wear plastic gloves when handling)

In a resealable plastic bag, combine the steak, lemon juice, soy sauce, garlic, ginger and peppers. Shake well. Refrigerate for 25 minutes or up to 24 hours, turning occasionally.

Remove the steak from the marinade and grill for 7 minutes per side, or until the meat is light pink when tested with a knife for medium-rare. Baste twice with the marinade while grilling; discard the remaining marinade.

To serve, slice thinly across the grain and on an angle.

PER SERVING

218 calories

8.2 g. fat
(35% of calories)

0 g. dietary fiber

50 mg. cholesterol

589 mg. sodium

PREPARATION TIME
5 minutes
plus 25 minutes
marinating time

COOKING TIME
14 minutes

PREPARATION TIME
10 minutes

COOKING TIME
15 minutes

Savory Beef Stew

serves 4

Pressure cooking produces old-fashioned beef stew in record time. It's great served with noodles and green peas.

¹/₄	cup all-purpose flour
¹/₂	teaspoon salt
¹/₄	teaspoon dry mustard
1	pound lean sirloin, trimmed of all visible fat and cubed
1¹/₂	teaspoons olive oil
¹/₂	cup defatted beef broth
1	can (14 ounces) tomatoes (with juice), chopped
1	cup diced red potatoes
¹/₂	cup diced onions
1	medium carrot, chopped
2	tablespoons minced garlic
2	tablespoons tomato paste
2	tablespoons balsamic vinegar
1	tablespoon brown sugar
1¹/₂	teaspoons dried thyme
2	bay leaves

In a resealable plastic bag, combine the flour, salt, mustard and sirloin. Shake well. Warm the oil in a pressure cooker over medium-high heat. Transfer the sirloin to the pan and brown on all sides.

Add the broth and bring to a boil, scraping the bottom of the pan to loosen any browned bits. Add the tomatoes (with juice), potatoes, onions, carrots, garlic, tomato paste, vinegar, brown sugar, thyme and bay leaves.

Lock the pressure cooker lid in place and bring to high pressure over high heat. Cook for 12 minutes. Release the pressure. Remove and discard the bay leaves.

Chef's Note

If you don't have a pressure cooker, use a Dutch oven. Increase the amount of beef broth to 3 cups and cook for 1¹/₂ to 2 hours over medium heat, stirring occasionally.

Beef Stroganoff

serves 4

Traditional stroganoff recipes are loaded with sour cream, making them really high in calories and fat. This version is much lighter but just as satisfying.

PER SERVING

449 calories

19 g. fat
(38% of calories)

2 g. dietary fiber

101 mg. cholesterol

720 mg. sodium

1	pound lean sirloin, trimmed of all visible fat and cut into strips
1/2	teaspoon salt
1/4	teaspoon dry mustard
1/4	cup plus 1 tablespoon all-purpose flour
2	teaspoons olive oil
1 1/2	cups defatted beef broth
2	tablespoons balsamic vinegar
1 1/2	teaspoons dried thyme
1	large onion, sliced
8	ounces mushrooms, sliced
2	tablespoons minced garlic
2	bay leaves
8	ounces sour cream
	Salt and ground black pepper
8	ounces noodles, cooked

PREPARATION TIME
10 minutes

COOKING TIME
15 minutes

In a resealable plastic bag, combine the sirloin, salt, mustard and 1/4 cup of the flour. Shake well.

Warm the oil in a large no-stick frying pan over medium-high heat. Shake excess flour off the beef and add the beef to the pan. Stir to brown on all sides. Transfer to a plate.

Add the broth, vinegar and thyme to the pan. Bring to a boil, scraping the bottom of the pan to loosen any browned bits. Add the onions, mushrooms, garlic and bay leaves. Cook, stirring frequently, for 5 minutes. Add the beef. Cover, reduce the heat to low and simmer for 5 minutes.

In a small bowl, stir together the sour cream and the remaining 1 tablespoon flour. Stir into the pan and heat through. Season with the salt and pepper to taste. Remove and discard the bay leaves. Serve over the noodles.

PREPARATION TIME
5 minutes
plus 30 minutes
marinating time

COOKING TIME
10 minutes

Pork BBQ Sandwiches

Serves 4

You don't need to spend the whole day slaving over the barbecue pit to enjoy the taste of real Texas-style barbecue.

1 pound boneless pork tenderloin, cut into 4 slices

1 tablespoon chopped chipotle chili peppers in adobo sauce

1 cup plus 1 tablespoon reduced-sodium barbecue sauce

8 slices thick Italian bread, grilled

In a resealable plastic bag, combine the pork, peppers and 1 cup of the barbecue sauce. Shake well. Refrigerate for 30 minutes or up to 24 hours, turning occasionally.

Grill the pork for 5 minutes per side, or until slightly charred and no longer pink when tested with a knife. Slice thin.

Lightly grill the buns and spread the cut sides with the remaining 1 tablespoon barbecue sauce. Top with the pork.

Oven-Fried Pepper-Dusted Potato Wedges recipe on page 168

Honey-Glazed Carrots recipe on page 174

Stuffed Pork Loin Chops

Serves 4

As good as slow-cooked pork roast but ready in a fraction of the time, these stuffed pork chops will satisfy the heartiest appetite.

4	thick-cut pork loin chops, trimmed of all visible fat
1½	cups dry cornbread stuffing
1	teaspoon poultry seasoning
¼	cup minced onions
2–2½	cups defatted chicken broth
2	tablespoons balsamic vinegar
1	teaspoon cornstarch
1	tablespoon water

Cut a slit in the side of each chop to form a pocket. In a small bowl, mix the stuffing, poultry seasoning, onions and ½ to 1 cup of the broth (enough to create a moist stuffing). Pack the stuffing into the pockets; seal the pockets shut with wooden toothpicks, if necessary.

Coat a large no-stick frying pan with no-stick cooking spray and place over medium-high heat for 2 minutes. Add the pork chops. Brown for 2 to 3 minutes per side. Add 1 cup of the remaining broth. Cover, reduce the heat to low and simmer for 25 minutes, or until the pork is tender and no longer pink when tested with a knife. Transfer to a plate.

Add the vinegar and the remaining ½ cup broth to the pan. Bring to a boil. In a cup, mix the cornstarch and water; add to the pan. Cook, stirring, until the broth has thickened; pour over the pork chops.

PER SERVING

272 calories

11.2 g. fat
(38% of calories)

0.2 g. dietary fiber

54 mg. cholesterol

368 mg. sodium

PREPARATION TIME
10 minutes

COOKING TIME
35 minutes

Meaty Entrées

Pulled Pork Barbecue

serves 4

You "pull" pork by shredding it with two forks. Serve this Southern-style barbecued pork on buns along with your favorite slaw, sliced tomatoes, corn on the cob and watermelon for a summer picnic.

PER SERVING

270 calories

6.4 g. fat
(22% of calories)

2.4 g. dietary fiber

60 mg. cholesterol

399 mg. sodium

PREPARATION TIME
10 minutes

COOKING TIME
45 minutes

1	chipotle pepper (wear plastic gloves when handling)
12	ounces pork tenderloin
$1/4$	teaspoon ground black pepper
$1/8$	teaspoon ground red pepper
$2/3$	cup diced onions
1	teaspoon canola oil
1	tablespoon minced garlic
$1/2$	cup barbecue sauce
$1/4$	cup ketchup
$1/4$	cup water
1	teaspoon maple syrup
4	sandwich buns, split and warmed

Place the chipotle pepper in a small bowl; cover with hot water and let stand for 5 minutes. Drain; remove the stem and seeds. Coarsely chop the pepper.

Coat a large no-stick frying pan with no-stick spray and warm over high heat. Add the pork and brown on all sides. Sprinkle with the black pepper and red pepper. Transfer to a large sheet of aluminum foil.

In a 2-quart saucepan over medium heat, sauté the onions in the oil for 5 minutes. Add the garlic and cook for 1 minute. Add the barbecue sauce, ketchup, water, maple syrup and chipotle peppers. Bring to a boil and simmer for 10 minutes.

Spoon one-third of the sauce over the pork. Wrap well and bake at 350° for 25 minutes, or until tender and no longer pink when tested with a knife.

Shred the pork using 2 forks. Add to the remaining sauce and heat through. Serve on the buns.

Chef's Note

Chipotle peppers are smoked and dried jalapeños. There is no substitute for the flavor they add, but a fresh serrano or jalapeño pepper can be used to add the same spiciness.

PREPARATION TIME
10 minutes

COOKING TIME
10 minutes

Lamb Chops
with Cucumbers and Tomatoes

serves 4

Fresh herbs, crisp cucumbers and sweet tomatoes play off the distinctive flavor of quickly seared lamb chops.

1	cup thinly sliced tomatoes
1	cup thinly sliced cucumbers
2	tablespoons orange juice
2	tablespoons chopped fresh mint
1	tablespoon chopped fresh rosemary
1	teaspoon grated orange rind
	Salt and ground black pepper
4	loin lamb chops (about 4 ounces each)

In a medium bowl, mix the tomatoes, cucumbers, orange juice, mint, rosemary and orange rind; add salt and pepper to taste.

Warm a large no-stick frying pan over medium-high heat. Add the lamb and sauté for 5 minutes per side, or until medium-rare. Serve with the tomato mixture.

PREPARATION TIME
10 minutes

COOKING TIME
30 minutes

Simmered Sauerkraut and Pork

serves 4

Bring Oktoberfest to your dining room when you serve this authentic German supper. Dark rye bread, chunky cinnamon-flavored applesauce and mashed potatoes topped with browned onions would complete the meal nicely.

$^{1}/_{2}$	cup dried apple slices
1	cup diced onions
3	strips turkey bacon, diced
1	teaspoon canola oil
2	cups sauerkraut, rinsed and drained
1	cup defatted chicken broth
$^{1}/_{8}$	teaspoon fennel seeds
$^{1}/_{8}$	teaspoon caraway seeds
4	pork chops (3 ounces each), trimmed of all visible fat

Place the apples in a small bowl; cover with hot water and let stand for 5 minutes. Drain.

In a Dutch oven over medium heat, sauté the onions and bacon in the oil for 5 minutes. Add the sauerkraut, broth, fennel seeds, caraway seeds and apples. Cover and simmer for 10 minutes.

Coat a large no-stick frying pan with no-stick spray and warm over medium heat. Add the pork chops and cook for 2 minutes per side, or until browned. Transfer to the Dutch oven. Cover and simmer for 10 minutes, or until the pork chops are cooked through and no longer pink when tested with a knife.

Meatless Meals

VEGETARIAN CASSEROLES, STIR-FRIES AND MORE

No-meat meals have become popular not only because they're economical but also because they're healthful. Vegetarian dishes bring stimulating variety to our diets through the creative use of vegetables, pasta and dried beans. Meatless meals are power-packed with complex carbohydrates, protein and fiber—and can be very low in fat, calories and cholesterol. Many of this chapter's main dishes are variations of American favorites, such as Eggplant Parmesan and Pasta Primavera, while others are delectable originals, like Chick-Pea Fritters with Pepper Sauce and Polenta with Mushroom-Tomato Sauce.

Polenta with Mushroom-Tomato Sauce

serves 4

PER SERVING

214 calories

5.9 g. fat
(24% of calories)

6.2 g. dietary fiber

2 mg. cholesterol

583 mg. sodium

PREPARATION TIME
10 minutes

COOKING TIME
30 minutes

Instant polenta makes this dish fast to prepare.

3½	cups vegetable broth
1	cup instant polenta
2	shallots, minced
2	teaspoons chopped fresh rosemary
1	tablespoon olive oil
4	cups thinly sliced mushrooms
1	cup canned crushed tomatoes
¼	cup white wine or tomato juice
1	tablespoon balsamic vinegar
2	tablespoons grated Parmesan cheese
2	tablespoons chopped fresh parsley
	Salt and ground black pepper

Bring the broth to a boil in a 2-quart saucepan over high heat. Reduce the heat to low and slowly whisk in the polenta. Cook, stirring occasionally, for 10 minutes, or until very thick.

In a large no-stick frying pan over medium heat, sauté the shallots and rosemary in the oil for 2 minutes. Stir in the mushrooms, tomatoes, wine or tomato juice and vinegar. Bring to a boil. Cover, reduce the heat and simmer for 5 minutes.

Uncover and cook for 15 to 20 minutes, or until the sauce thickens. Stir in the Parmesan and parsley; add salt and pepper to taste. Serve over the polenta.

Chef's Note

You can easily make this recipe ahead. Pour the cooked polenta into a loaf pan. Cover and refrigerate. To use, cut into 2" slices, place on a baking sheet and bake at 400° for 10 minutes, or until golden brown. Reheat the sauce and serve over the polenta slices.

PREPARATION TIME
5 minutes

COOKING TIME
12 minutes

Noodles with Low-Fat Peanut Sauce

serves 4

Try these Asian noodles for a fast and fabulous lunch. Look for udon noodles in the international section of the supermarket.

1	package (9 ounces) Japanese udon noodles
1	tablespoon reduced-sodium soy sauce
2	teaspoons peanut butter
2	teaspoons honey
1	teaspoon minced scallions
1	teaspoon water
1/2	teaspoon minced garlic

Cook the noodles in a large pot of boiling water according to the package directions. Drain.

In a large bowl, whisk together the soy sauce, peanut butter, honey, scallions, and water. Add the noodles and toss to mix.

Eggplant Cheese Quesadillas

serves 4

Cheese lovers will eat up these easy tortilla "sandwiches."

1	cup diced peeled eggplant
1/2	cup diced tomatoes
1/3	cup chopped scallions
1/4	cup apple juice
1	cup shredded reduced-fat Monterey Jack cheese
1/2	cup fat-free sour cream
1/4	cup grated Parmesan cheese
8	large flour tortillas

In a large no-stick frying pan, combine the eggplant, tomatoes, scallions and apple juice. Cover and cook over medium-high heat for 3 minutes, or until the vegetables are soft. Uncover and cook for 5 minutes, or until the liquid has evaporated.

In a small bowl, combine the Monterey Jack, sour cream and Parmesan. Spread on 4 of the tortillas. Top with the vegetables. Cover with the remaining tortillas.

Wash the frying pan and place over medium heat. Cook each quesadilla for 1 minute per side, or until the cheese melts. Cut into wedges.

PER SERVING

285 calories

7.1 g. fat
(20% of calories)

11.3 g. dietary fiber

25 mg. cholesterol

930 mg. sodium

PREPARATION TIME
10 minutes

COOKING TIME
20 minutes

Vegetable Pizza with Goat Cheese

serves 4

PER SERVING

375 calories

10.1 g. fat
(24% of calories)

2.9 g. dietary fiber

11 mg. cholesterol

668 mg. sodium

Here's a homemade pie that's in the oven in 10 minutes. The secret is precut vegetables, prepared pizza dough and bought pesto.

1	teaspoon cornmeal
1	pound refrigerated pizza dough
2	tablespoons pesto
1	red onion, thinly sliced
1	large tomato, sliced
1	jar (7 ounces) roasted sweet red peppers, drained
1	cup chopped broccoli florets
$1/3$	cup crumbled goat cheese
2	tablespoons grated Parmesan cheese

PREPARATION TIME
10 minutes

BAKING TIME
15 minutes

Sprinkle the cornmeal on a pizza pan or large baking sheet. Roll out the dough and place it on the sheet, pressing to fit.

Spread the pesto on the dough; top with the onions and tomatoes. Sprinkle with the peppers, broccoli, goat cheese and Parmesan. Bake at 500° for 10 to 15 minutes, or until the crust is browned and the cheese has melted.

PREPARATION TIME
10 minutes

BAKING TIME
12 minutes

Greengrocer's Pizza

serves 4

Bet you've never had this before. It's a fresh, crispy salad served up in a pizza shell. Popular in trattorias throughout Italy, its success relies on very fresh ingredients.

Crust

1	teaspoon cornmeal
1	pound refrigerated pizza dough
¼	cup shredded provolone cheese

Vegetable Topping

2	tablespoons olive oil
2	teaspoons chopped fresh oregano
1	teaspoon balsamic vinegar
1	teaspoon lemon juice
2	plum tomatoes, cubed
2	tablespoons chopped red onions
2	tablespoons chopped fresh basil
	Salt and ground black pepper
6	cups mixed lettuce

TO MAKE THE CRUST

Sprinkle the cornmeal on a large baking sheet. Divide the dough into 4 pieces and form each into a 6" round. Place on the sheet. Prick the dough deeply all over with a fork.

Bake at 500° for 10 minutes, or until the crusts turn golden brown. Remove from the oven and sprinkle with the provolone. Bake for 2 minutes, or until the provolone melts. Remove the crusts from the oven.

TO MAKE THE VEGETABLE TOPPING

In a large bowl, whisk together the oil, oregano, vinegar and lemon juice. Stir in the tomatoes, onions and basil; add salt and pepper to taste.

Just before serving, add the lettuce to the tomato mixture and toss to coat. Divide the mixture evenly over the crusts.

PREPARATION TIME
5 minutes

COOKING TIME
10 minutes

Bean and Grain Patties

serves 4

When you're in the mood for burgers but don't want to eat meat, try these inventive look-alikes.

1	can (16 ounces) chick-peas, rinsed and drained
2	eggs
1/3	cup shredded reduced-fat Cheddar cheese
1/4	cup cooked rice
3/4	cup dry bread crumbs
2	tablespoons chopped fresh parsley
3	cloves garlic, minced
2	scallions, chopped
4	pitas
1	tomato, thinly sliced
4	large leaves lettuce
1/2	cup prepared hummus

Using a fork, mash the chick-peas in a medium bowl. Stir in the eggs, Cheddar, rice, bread crumbs, parsley, garlic and scallions.

Coat a large no-stick frying pan with no-stick spray. Using a large spoon, divide the chick-pea mixture into 8 patties (the mixture will be wet); transfer to the frying pan. Cook over medium-high heat for 5 minutes, then turn and flatten with a spatula. Cook for 3 to 5 minutes, or until firm and lightly browned.

Trim one edge off each pita. Open the pitas along the rim and tuck in the patties, tomatoes and lettuce. Top with the hummus.

Meatless Meals

Lemon-Chive Ravioli

serves 4

PER SERVING

189 calories

5.1 g. fat
(24% of calories)

0 g. dietary fiber

24 mg. cholesterol

303 mg. sodium

Ready-made cheese ravioli is available in most markets and cooks in minutes. For an unusual flavor, top it with a lemony white sauce. Serve with breadsticks and a tossed salad.

PREPARATION TIME
5 minutes

COOKING TIME
15 minutes

2	tablespoons all-purpose flour
1½	cups skim milk
1	tablespoon chopped fresh chives
1	teaspoon grated lemon rind
½	teaspoon minced fresh rosemary
4	tablespoons grated Parmesan cheese
9	ounces cheese ravioli

Place the flour in a 2-quart saucepan. Gradually whisk in the milk until smooth. Whisk in the chives, lemon rind, rosemary and 2 tablespoons of the Parmesan. Whisk over medium heat for 5 minutes, or until the mixture comes to a boil and thickens.

Cook the ravioli in a large pot of boiling water according to the package directions. Drain. Serve topped with the sauce and sprinkled with the remaining 2 tablespoons Parmesan.

PREPARATION TIME
5 minutes

COOKING TIME
10 minutes

Pasta Primavera

serves 4

Primavera means "springtime" in Italian. This dish is a medley of fresh spring flavors. You can vary your selection of vegetables with the season.

12	ounces angel hair pasta
3	cloves garlic, minced
1	teaspoon olive oil
1	cup broccoli florets
1/4	cup white wine or vegetable broth
1	sweet red pepper, cut into 1" pieces
1	green pepper, cut into1" pieces
1	medium zucchini, julienned
1	large carrot, julienned
1/4	cup chopped fresh basil
2	tablespoons shredded Parmesan cheese

Cook the angel hair in a large pot of boiling water according to the package directions. Drain.

In a large no-stick frying pan over medium heat, sauté the garlic in the oil for 1 minute. Add the broccoli and wine or broth; cover and cook for 1 minute.

Add the red peppers, green peppers, zucchini, carrots and basil; cover and cook for 1 minute, or until the vegetables are crisp-tender. Uncover and cook for 1 minute, or until the liquid is reduced. Add the angel hair and toss. Sprinkle with the Parmesan.

PREPARATION TIME
10 minutes

COOKING TIME
15 minutes

Lean Fettuccine Alfredo

serves 4

Most recipes for fettuccine Alfredo give you more than a whole day's worth of fat in a single serving. We've kept this recipe nice and light with reduced-fat dairy products.

8	ounces fettuccine
½	cup fat-free cottage cheese
¼	cup evaporated skim milk
¼	cup reduced-fat ricotta cheese
¼	cup shredded reduced-fat Monterey Jack cheese
¼	cup grated Parmesan cheese
1	teaspoon minced garlic
2	tablespoons minced parsley

Cook the fettuccine in a large pot of boiling water according to the package directions. Drain.

In a blender or food processor, process the cottage cheese, milk and ricotta until smooth. Transfer to a large no-stick frying pan and add the Monterey Jack, Parmesan and garlic. Stir over medium heat for 3 to 5 minutes, or until the cheeses are melted and the sauce is smooth.

Add the fettuccine and toss to coat. Heat through. Sprinkle with the parsley.

30-Minute Manicotti

serves 4

PER SERVING

332 calories

6.8 g. fat
(19% of calories)

2.1 g. dietary fiber

74 mg. cholesterol

568 mg. sodium

Who'd believe real Italian manicotti could be this quick? Part of the secret is cooking the assembled dish in the microwave.

8	manicotti shells
2	cups reduced-fat ricotta cheese
1	cup finely chopped spinach
1	egg
1/4	cup grated Parmesan cheese
2	tablespoons minced fresh basil
1/4	cup chopped fresh parsley
1/4	teaspoon ground nutmeg
2	cups tomato sauce
1 1/2	cups shredded fat-free mozzarella cheese

PREPARATION TIME
15 minutes

COOKING TIME
15 minutes

Cook the manicotti in a large pot of boiling water according to the package directions. Drain and transfer to a bowl of cold water.

In a medium bowl, mix the ricotta, spinach, egg, Parmesan, basil, parsley and nutmeg. Drain the manicotti shells and fill each with about 1/4 cup of the mixture.

Spoon 1 cup of the tomato sauce into an 11" × 7" microwave-safe baking dish. Arrange the shells in the pan; spoon the remaining 1 cup tomato sauce on top. Sprinkle with the mozzarella. Cover with vented plastic wrap.

Microwave on medium-high (70% power) for 15 minutes, or until the sauce is bubbling; rotate the dish every 5 minutes during cooking.

Mediterranean Penne

serves 4

Feta cheese and toasted pine nuts give this dish a decidedly Greek flavor.
Use your choice of greens, such as escarole, kale and arugula.

10	ounces penne pasta
1	small onion, chopped
2	cloves garlic, minced
1	tablespoon olive oil
4	cups mixed chopped bitter greens
1/4	cup vegetable broth
2	tomatoes, chopped
	Salt and ground black pepper
1/4	cup crumbled feta cheese
1/4	cup toasted pine nuts

Cook the penne in a large pot of boiling water according to the package directions. Drain and place in a large bowl.

In a large no-stick frying pan over medium-high heat, sauté the onions and garlic in the oil for 5 minutes, or until soft. Add the greens and sauté for 1 minute. Add the broth and cook for 1 minute, or until the greens are wilted. Add the tomatoes and salt and pepper to taste.

Toss the greens mixture with the penne. Serve sprinkled with the feta and pine nuts.

PER SERVING

445 calories

14.4 g. fat
(29% of calories)

7.4 g. dietary fiber

8 mg. cholesterol

169 mg. sodium

PREPARATION TIME
5 minutes

COOKING TIME
15 minutes

PREPARATION TIME
10 minutes

BAKING TIME
30 minutes

Spaghetti with Eggplant and Tomatoes

serves 4

This dish is from Sicily, where abundant eggplant is added to numerous tomato dishes. Often the eggplant is fried; here it is baked to keep fat low.

1	medium eggplant, peeled and cut into $1/2$" slices
1	tablespoon plus 1 teaspoon olive oil
10	ounces spaghetti
$1/2$	cup minced onions
5	cloves garlic, minced
$1 1/2$	pounds plum tomatoes, chopped
$1/4$	cup grated Parmesan cheese
	Salt and ground black pepper
$1/4$	cup chopped fresh basil

Coat a 13" × 9" baking dish with no-stick spray. Add the eggplant. Drizzle with 1 tablespoon of the oil. Cover with aluminum foil and bake at 450° for 25 to 30 minutes, or until tender.

Cook the spaghetti in a large pot of boiling water according to the package directions. Drain.

In a large no-stick frying pan over medium heat, sauté the onions and garlic in the remaining 1 teaspoon oil for 1 minute. Add the tomatoes; cover and cook for 2 minutes, or until soft. Uncover and cook for 2 minutes.

Stir in the eggplant, spaghetti and Parmesan. Add salt and pepper to taste. Toss to mix. Sprinkle with the basil.

PREPARATION TIME
10 minutes

BAKING TIME
40 minutes

Eggplant Parmesan

serves 4

Eggplant Parmesan is usually high in fat because traditional recipes call for sautéing the eggplant in lots of oil. Here, we bake the eggplant.

2	medium eggplants
4	egg whites
$^1/_2$	cup dry bread crumbs
$^1/_2$	teaspoon dried basil
$^1/_2$	teaspoon dried oregano
$^1/_2$	teaspoon garlic powder
$^1/_4$	teaspoon ground black pepper
3	cups tomato sauce
8	ounces fat-free mozzarella cheese, shredded
$^1/_4$	cup grated Parmesan cheese
2	tablespoons chopped fresh parsley

Cut the eggplants crosswise into $^1/_2$" slices.

Place the egg whites in a shallow bowl and beat lightly with a fork. On a sheet of wax paper, mix the bread crumbs, basil, oregano, garlic powder and pepper.

Dip each eggplant slice first into the egg whites, then into the crumb mixture to coat both sides. Place on a no-stick baking sheet and broil about 4" from the heat for 5 minutes per side, or until lightly browned.

Spread about $^1/_2$ cup of the tomato sauce in the bottom of a 13" × 9" baking dish. Arrange a layer of eggplant slices on top. Sprinkle with some of the mozzarella and Parmesan. Repeat layering, ending with tomato sauce, until all the ingredients have been used. Sprinkle with the parsley.

Cover and bake at 350° for 30 minutes.

Baked Macaroni and Cheese

serves 4

PER SERVING

415 calories

10.8 g. fat
(24% of calories)

0.2 g. dietary fiber

24 mg. cholesterol

606 mg. sodium

Here's a new twist on a classic dinner. And it takes only about a half-hour to get it on the table.

8	ounces elbow macaroni
1	tablespoon olive oil
1	tablespoon all-purpose flour
$\frac{1}{2}$	teaspoon dry mustard
$1\frac{1}{4}$	cups skim milk
$1\frac{1}{4}$	cups shredded reduced-fat Cheddar cheese
2	tablespoons chopped scallions
$\frac{1}{4}$	teaspoon ground black pepper
$\frac{1}{2}$	cup reduced-fat ricotta cheese
$\frac{1}{4}$	cup dry bread crumbs

PREPARATION TIME
10 minutes

BAKING TIME
20 minutes

Cook the macaroni in a large pot of boiling water according to the package directions. Drain and place in a large bowl.

In a 2-quart saucepan, whisk together the oil, flour and mustard. Stir over medium heat for 1 minute. Gradually whisk in the milk. Cook, stirring, for 5 minutes, or until thickened. Stir in the Cheddar, scallions and pepper. Pour over the macaroni and stir well.

In a blender or food processor, process the ricotta until very smooth. Add to the bowl and mix well.

Coat an 11" × 7" baking dish with no-stick spray. Add the macaroni mixture. Top with the bread crumbs. Bake at 375° for 20 minutes, or until the top is golden brown.

Meatless Meals

Grilled Vegetable Pasta with Red-Pepper Sauce

serves 4

PER SERVING

95 calories

2.7 g. fat
(23% of calories)

3.4 g. dietary fiber

5 mg. cholesterol

246 mg. sodium

PREPARATION TIME
10 minutes

COOKING TIME
20 minutes

There's nothing shy or subtle about this color-splashed pasta dish.
Grilling adds a smoky taste to the vegetables, but they also may be broiled.

8	ounces rigatoni pasta
2	medium zucchini
2	medium yellow summer squash
2	fennel bulbs, cut into wedges
1	red onion, sliced into $1/4$" rings
2	tablespoons chopped fresh rosemary
1	jar (7 ounces) roasted sweet red peppers, drained
$1/2$	cup vegetable broth
$1/2$	teaspoon ground red pepper
$1/4$	cup grated Parmesan cheese

Cook the rigatoni in a large pot of boiling water according to the package directions. Drain and place in a large bowl.

Cut the zucchini and the squash into $1/4$"-thick diagonal slices. Coat the zucchini, squash, fennel and onions with no-stick spray and sprinkle with the rosemary. Grill for 3 minutes per side, or until golden.

In a blender, process the red peppers, broth and ground red pepper until smooth. Transfer to a 1-quart saucepan and warm over medium heat. Pour over the rigatoni and toss well.

Top with the grilled vegetables and sprinkle with the Parmesan.

PREPARATION TIME
15 minutes

COOKING TIME
20 minutes

Chick-Pea Fritters with Pepper Sauce

serves 4

Serve these fritters for dinner or even for brunch.

1	jar (7 ounces) roasted sweet red peppers, drained and chopped
1	tomato, diced
1	clove garlic, minced
2	teaspoons balsamic vinegar
1/4	teaspoon honey
1 3/4	cups rinsed and drained canned chick-peas
1	small sweet potato, peeled and finely shredded
1/4	cup finely chopped scallions
1	tablespoon all-purpose flour
2	teaspoons lemon juice
	Pinch of ground black pepper
1/2	cup fat-free egg substitute
2	tablespoons olive oil

In a small bowl, mix the red peppers, tomatoes, garlic, vinegar and honey.

In a medium bowl, coarsely mash the chick-peas with a fork.

In a large bowl, mix the sweet potatoes, scallions, flour, lemon juice and black pepper. Stir in the chick-peas and egg substitute.

Warm 1 tablespoon of the oil in a large no-stick frying pan over medium heat. Drop rounded tablespoonfuls of the chick-pea mixture into the pan, allowing room for them to spread. Cook for 3 minutes per side, or until lightly browned and cooked through. Transfer to a platter and keep warm. Continue making fritters, adding more oil as needed. Serve with the pepper mixture.

Classic Accompaniments

ALL-TIME FAVORITE SIDE DISHES

Think of a meal's main dish as the star and the side dishes as the supporting cast. They make the star look (and in this case, taste) great, but they can also earn some applause on their own. Side dishes enhance the entrée by providing contrasting or complementary flavors, colors and textures. They also bolster the healthful benefit of a meal by adding nutrients that the main dish lacks. Here are classic accompaniments that are easy to prepare and will complement everything from meat loaf to grilled salmon steaks.

Cheesy Twice-Baked Potatoes

serves 4

Everybody loves twice-baked potatoes. And you'll feel good about serving them when they're this low in fat.

PER SERVING

134 calories

0.4 g. fat
(3% of calories)

1.6 g. dietary fiber

0 mg. cholesterol

47 mg. sodium

PREPARATION TIME
20 minutes

BAKING TIME
5 minutes

4	medium russet potatoes
2	tablespoons minced onions
3	tablespoons fat-free sour cream
1	tablespoon chopped fresh parsley
	Pinch of ground black pepper
1	tablespoon shredded reduced-fat Cheddar cheese
1/4	teaspoon paprika

Pierce the potatoes in several places with a fork and microwave on high power for 7 to 10 minutes, turning once, or until the potatoes are tender. Let stand for 5 minutes, or until cool enough to handle.

Coat a small no-stick frying pan with no-stick spray and warm over medium heat. Add the onions and sauté for 3 to 4 minutes, or until lightly browned.

Slice 1/4" off the top of each potato and scoop out the center with a spoon, leaving a 1/4"-thick shell. Place the centers in a medium bowl and mash with a fork. Stir in the onions, sour cream, parsley and pepper.

Spoon the filling into the potato shells and top with the Cheddar. Sprinkle with the paprika.

Place the potatoes on a baking sheet and bake at 475° for 3 to 5 minutes, or until the filling is hot and the Cheddar has melted.

Classic Accompaniments

Apple-Walnut Stuffing

serves 8

If you love stuffing but hate the large serving of fat you get with most types, try this lighter version. Serve as an accompaniment to roast poultry or even simple sautéed chicken breasts.

PER SERVING

225 calories

11 g. fat
(44% of calories)

3.2 g. dietary fiber

0 mg. cholesterol

198 mg. sodium

PREPARATION TIME
15 minutes

BAKING TIME
45 minutes

2	onions, chopped
4	stalks celery, sliced
1	medium carrot, shredded
1	tablespoon olive oil
1$\frac{1}{4}$	cups defatted chicken broth
$\frac{1}{4}$	cup fat-free egg substitute
2	medium apples, chopped
$\frac{1}{2}$	cup walnuts, coarsely chopped
3	tablespoons chopped fresh parsley
1	teaspoon dried rosemary
$\frac{1}{4}$	teaspoon ground black pepper
6$\frac{1}{2}$	cups bread cubes

In a 3-quart saucepan over medium-high heat, sauté the onions, celery and carrots in the oil for 5 minutes, or until soft. Remove from the heat. Stir in the broth, egg substitute, apples, walnuts, parsley, rosemary and pepper. Add the bread cubes and mix well.

Coat a 13" × 9" baking dish with no-stick spray. Add the stuffing. Cover with aluminum foil and bake at 325° for 45 minutes, or until browned.

Classic Accompaniments

Asparagus with Roasted Peppers and Olives

serves 4

PER SERVING

52 calories

1.8 g. fat
(27% of calories)

0.4 g. dietary fiber

4 mg. cholesterol

43 mg. sodium

A lively dish that's wonderful alongside grilled or broiled pork or chicken. Tossed with pasta, it becomes a light meal. It is equally good hot or at room temperature.

PREPARATION TIME
5 minutes

COOKING TIME
5 minutes

1	pound asparagus, cut into 1" pieces
2	cloves garlic, minced
2	tablespoons lemon juice
1	jar (3½ ounces) chopped roasted sweet red peppers, drained
2	tablespoons chopped pitted black olives
1	tablespoon chopped fresh parsley
	Dash of hot–pepper sauce
	Salt and ground black pepper
2	tablespoons shredded provolone cheese

Coat a large no-stick frying pan with no-stick spray. Add the asparagus and garlic; stir over medium-high heat for 1 minute. Add the lemon juice. Cover and cook for 2 minutes, or until the asparagus is bright green and crisp-tender.

Stir in the red peppers, olives, parsley and hot-pepper sauce. Add salt and black pepper to taste. Sprinkle with the provolone.

PREPARATION TIME
15 minutes

COOKING TIME
11 minutes

Marinated Vegetables

serves 8

You can make this dish a day or two ahead so the vegetables absorb the marinade and the flavors have time to blend. Serve chilled or at room temperature.

Marinade

½	cup white wine vinegar
1	tablespoon olive oil
1	teaspoon lemon juice
1	teaspoon Dijon mustard
1	teaspoon sugar
1	clove garlic, minced
2	tablespoons chopped fresh marjoram
2	tablespoons chopped fresh parsley

Vegetables

8	ounces new potatoes, cubed
1	cup broccoli florets
1	sweet red pepper, cut into 2" pieces
1	cup quartered mushrooms
½	cup sliced scallions
2	tablespoons sliced pitted black olives
	Salt and ground black pepper

TO MAKE THE MARINADE

In a large bowl, whisk together the vinegar, oil, lemon juice, mustard, sugar and garlic. Stir in the marjoram and parsley,

TO MAKE THE VEGETABLES

In a large microwave-safe dish, microwave the potatoes on high power for 8 minutes, or until tender. Add to the marinade while still hot.

In the same microwave-safe dish, microwave the broccoli for 3 minutes, or until crisp-tender. Add to the marinade. Stir in the peppers, mushrooms, scallions and olives. Add salt and black pepper to taste.

Spicy Corn on the Cob

serves 4

Prepare this corn anytime you're having a cookout. It can grill in its own foil packet while your main dish is cooking.

PER SERVING

155 calories

4.3 g. fat
(22% of calories)

2.7 g. dietary fiber

0 mg. cholesterol

6 mg. sodium

PREPARATION TIME
5 minutes

COOKING TIME
20 minutes

Photo on page 74

4	ears corn, shucked
2	tablespoons balsamic vinegar
1	tablespoon olive oil
¼	teaspoon ground red pepper

Place the corn on a large sheet of aluminum foil.

In a small bowl, stir together the vinegar, oil and pepper. Brush on the corn. Seal the foil tightly. Grill for 20 minutes, or until the corn is cooked through; turn the packet after 10 minutes.

Oven-Fried Pepper-Dusted Potato Wedges

Serves 4

They're wonderful steak fries, but they're virtually fat-free since they aren't deep-fried.

PER SERVING

220 calories

0.2 g. fat
(1% of calories)

2.2 g. dietary fiber

0 mg. cholesterol

16 mg. sodium

PREPARATION TIME
10 minutes

COOKING TIME
20 minutes

Photo on page 125

4	medium russet potatoes
	Ground red pepper
	Salt and ground black pepper

Pierce the potatoes in several places with a fork and microwave on high power for 7 to 10 minutes, turning once, or until the potatoes are tender. Let stand for 5 minutes, or until cool enough to handle.

Cut each potato into 8 wedges and place on a baking sheet. Mist with no-stick spray and lightly sprinkle with the red pepper, salt and black pepper. Bake at 475° for 20 minutes, or until the potatoes are crisp and brown.

Garlic Mashed Potatoes

serves 4

PER SERVING

145 calories

0.2 g. fat
(1% of calories)

1.5 g. dietary fiber

0 mg. cholesterol

38 mg. sodium

There's virtually no fat in these wonderfully creamy potatoes. We've eliminated the fat by replacing the usual butter and heavy cream with fat-free sour cream and skim milk.

4	medium potatoes, peeled and cubed
6	cloves garlic
$1/3$	cup skim milk
$1/4$	cup fat-free sour cream

PREPARATION TIME
5 minutes

COOKING TIME
15 minutes

Place the potatoes and garlic in a 3-quart saucepan and add cold water to cover. Bring to a boil over high heat. Reduce the heat to medium and cook for 15 minutes, or until the potatoes are tender.

Drain well and return the mixture to the pan. Off heat, mash with a potato masher until smooth. Add the milk and stir over medium heat for 1 minute. Stir in the sour cream.

PREPARATION TIME
5 minutes

COOKING TIME
15 minutes

Garlicky Green Beans

serves 4

Don't be concerned about the amount of garlic used here. Boiling mellows and sweetens its distinctive flavor.

6	cloves garlic
1	pound green beans
2	tablespoons lemon juice
1	teaspoon olive oil
$1/8$	teaspoon ground black pepper

Bring a large pot of water to a boil over medium-high heat. Add the garlic and cook for 10 minutes, or until the garlic is tender when pierced with the tip of a knife. Remove with a slotted spoon and place in a small bowl.

Add the beans to the water. Cook for 5 minutes, or until the beans are crisp-tender. Drain and return the beans to the pot.

Mash the garlic with a fork. Stir in the lemon juice, oil and pepper. Pour over the beans and toss to coat.

Chef's Note

To easily remove the skin from a clove of garlic, cut the root end off and firmly press the flat side of a wide knife blade on the clove. The skin will loosen and the clove will easily slip out. This same technique can be used to ease mincing once the clove is peeled.

PREPARATION TIME
5 minutes

COOKING TIME
25 minutes

Molasses Baked Beans

serves 4

Baked beans are an all-American dish. To create a lighter version, we used reduced-fat turkey sausage rather than bacon. Although they're cooked on top of the stove to save time, these beans retain their baked-all-day flavor.

$1/3$	cup reduced-fat turkey sausage
$3/4$	cup diced onions
1	can ($14\frac{1}{2}$ ounces) pinto beans, rinsed and drained
$1/4$	cup molasses
3	tablespoons chili sauce
2	teaspoons Worcestershire sauce

Crumble the sausage into a 2-quart saucepan. Cook over medium heat for 3 minutes, breaking up the sausage with a wooden spoon. Add the onions and cook for 3 to 4 minutes, or until the onions are translucent.

Stir in the beans, molasses, chili sauce and Worcestershire sauce. Bring to a boil, reduce the heat to medium-low and cook for 10 to 15 minutes, or until the sauce has thickened.

Honey-Glazed Carrots

Serves 4

Give ordinary carrots extraordinary flavor with this sweet-tart glaze. They're a great accompaniment to most any meat or poultry main course.

- 1 cup orange juice
- 1 pound baby carrots
- 1 tablespoon balsamic vinegar
- 1 tablespoon honey

Bring the orange juice to a boil in a large no-stick frying pan over medium-high heat. Add the carrots. Reduce the heat to medium, cover and cook for 10 minutes, or until the carrots are tender. Stir in the vinegar and honey. Stir over medium-high heat for 3 minutes, or until most of the liquid has evaporated and the carrots are lightly glazed.

PREPARATION TIME
3 minutes

COOKING TIME
15 minutes

Photo on page 126

Corn Pudding

serves 4

This old-fashioned soufflé has its roots in New England and is a classic accompaniment for roasts, wild game, lobster or clams.

- 1 package (10 ounces) frozen corn, thawed
- 1 cup fat-free egg substitute
- 1/4 cup all-purpose flour
- 3 tablespoons maple syrup

In a blender, combine the corn, egg substitute, flour and maple syrup. Blend on high speed for 20 to 25 seconds, or until the corn is finely chopped.

Coat a 1-quart casserole with no-stick spray. Add the corn mixture. Bake at 425° for 25 to 30 minutes, or until slightly puffed and a knife inserted into the center comes out clean.

PREPARATION TIME
5 minutes

BAKING TIME
30 minutes

Barley Pilaf

serves 4

PER SERVING

170 calories

2.7 g. fat
(13% of calories)

5.4 g. dietary fiber

0 mg. cholesterol

52 mg. sodium

This satisfying side dish uses quick-cooking barley, which is ready in a fraction of the time needed for regular pearl barley. Serve the pilaf with sautéed chicken breasts or pork tenderloin cutlets.

PREPARATION TIME
5 minutes

COOKING TIME
20 minutes

2	cups defatted chicken broth
1	cup quick-cooking barley
1	bay leaf
1	cup diced carrots
1	onion, diced
1/4	cup sliced scallions
1	clove garlic, minced
1	teaspoon olive oil

In a 2-quart saucepan over medium-high heat, bring the broth, barley and bay leaf to a boil. Cover and cook over medium-low heat for 15 minutes, or until the barley is tender and the liquid has been absorbed. Remove and discard the bay leaf. Fluff the barley with a fork.

In a large no-stick frying pan over medium heat, sauté the carrots, onions, scallions and garlic in the oil for 5 minutes, or until the vegetables are just tender. Add the barley and toss to combine.

PREPARATION TIME
5 minutes

COOKING TIME
10 minutes

Celebration Rice

serves 4

Any occasion will be cause for celebration if you serve this festive dish.

1¼	cups quick-cooking brown rice
1	cup water
⅓	cup orange juice
1	tablespoon reduced-sodium soy sauce
1½	teaspoons olive oil
1	teaspoon grated orange rind
1	teaspoon curry powder
1	tablespoon toasted sesame seeds
2	tablespoons chopped fresh chives
2	tablespoons diced sweet red peppers

In a 2-quart saucepan over medium-high heat, bring the rice, water, orange juice, soy sauce, oil, orange rind and curry powder to a boil. Cover, reduce the heat to medium-low and simmer for 10 minutes, or until all the liquid has been absorbed.

Fluff the rice with a fork. Stir in the sesame seeds, chives and peppers.

Baked Goodies

FRESH FROM THE OVEN OR GRIDDLE

Wake up to a breakfast of crisp waffles, dress up a main dish with a round focaccia bread piping hot from the oven or make an open-faced sandwich on a slice of home-baked bread. You can enjoy these goodies even as you pare fat from your diet. Ingredients such as skim milk, buttermilk and fat-free sour cream greatly reduce the fat without compromising the flavor of these baked treats. We've adapted a whole bakery full of tempting favorites such as pound cake, cheesecake, bread pudding and muffins to fit your lower-fat lifestyle.

Country-Style Blueberry Muffins

makes 12

These streusel-topped muffins have a tender crumb with minimal fat.

PER MUFFIN

147 calories

2.9 g. fat
(17% of calories)

1.2 g. dietary fiber

21 mg. cholesterol

186 mg. sodium

2	tablespoons + 1½ cups all-purpose flour
2	tablespoons packed brown sugar
½	teaspoon ground cinnamon
1	tablespoon cold butter or margarine, cut into small pieces
½	cup sugar
2	teaspoons baking powder
½	teaspoon salt
½	cup skim milk
3	tablespoons fat-free vanilla yogurt
1	egg
1	tablespoon canola oil
1	teaspoon vanilla
½	teaspoon grated lemon rind
1½	cups blueberries

PREPARATION TIME
10 minutes

BAKING TIME
20 minutes

In a small bowl, mix 2 tablespoons of the flour, brown sugar, and cinnamon. With 2 knives, cut in the butter or margarine until the mixture resembles coarse meal. Set aside.

Preheat the oven to 400°. Coat a 12-cup muffin pan with no-stick spray.

In a large bowl, whisk together the remaining 1½ cups flour, sugar, baking powder, and salt.

In a medium bowl, whisk together the milk, yogurt, egg, oil, vanilla and lemon rind. Pour over the flour mixture and stir just until combined; do not overmix. Gently stir in the blueberries.

Divide the batter evenly among the muffins cups, filling them two-thirds full. Sprinkle each muffin with 1 teaspoon of the topping.

Bake for 17 to 20 minutes, or until a toothpick inserted in the center of a muffin comes out clean. Cool on a wire rack for 5 minutes before removing from the pan.

PREPARATION TIME
15 minutes

BAKING TIME
25 minutes

Bran Muffins

makes 12

Most bran muffins are high in fat, despite their reputation as a health food. In our version, skim milk and egg whites keep the muffins light, while whole-wheat flour and bran cereal give them a hearty texture and delicious flavor.

$1/2$	cup all-purpose flour
$1/2$	cup whole-wheat flour
1	tablespoon baking powder
$1/4$	teaspoon salt
$1/4$	teaspoon ground cinnamon
1	cup skim milk
2	tablespoons canola oil
2	tablespoons honey
3	egg whites
1	cup All-Bran cereal

Preheat the oven to 400°. Coat a 12-cup muffin pan with no-stick spray.

In a large bowl, whisk together the all-purpose flour, whole-wheat flour, baking powder, salt and cinnamon.

In a medium bowl, whisk together the milk, oil, honey and egg whites. Stir in the cereal and let stand for 10 minutes. Pour over the flour mixture and stir just until combined; do not overmix.

Divide the batter evenly among the muffin cups, filling them two-thirds full.

Bake for 20 to 25 minutes, or until a toothpick inserted in the center of a muffin comes out clean. Cool on a wire rack for 5 minutes before removing from the pan.

Spiced Pumpkin Bread

makes 1 loaf; 18 slices

A mixture of spices gives this quick bread real pumpkin pie flavor. Add $^1/_3$ cup chopped walnuts to add a nutty flavor to your bread.

1$^1/_2$	cups all-purpose flour
2	tablespoons cornstarch
$^3/_4$	teaspoon baking powder
$^1/_2$	teaspoon baking soda
$^1/_4$	teaspoon salt
$^1/_8$	teaspoon ground allspice
$^1/_8$	teaspoon ground cloves
$^1/_4$	teaspoon ground cinnamon
$^1/_4$	teaspoon ground nutmeg
1	egg
1	egg white
$^1/_3$	cup sugar
$^1/_4$	cup packed brown sugar
1	cup canned pumpkin
6	tablespoons low-fat buttermilk
1$^1/_2$	tablespoons canola oil
$^1/_2$	teaspoon vanilla

PER SLICE

91 calories

1.6 g. fat
(15% of calories)

0.7 g. dietary fiber

12 mg. cholesterol

92 mg. sodium

PREPARATION TIME
10 minutes

BAKING TIME
45 minutes

Preheat the oven to 350°. Coat a 9" × 5" loaf pan with no-stick spray.

In a large bowl, whisk together the flour, cornstarch, baking powder, baking soda, salt, allspice, cloves, cinnamon and nutmeg.

In a medium bowl, whisk together the egg, egg white, sugar and brown sugar until smooth. Whisk in the pumpkin, buttermilk, oil and vanilla. Pour over the flour mixture and stir just until combined; do not overmix.

Spoon the batter into the pan. Bake for 45 minutes, or until a toothpick inserted in the center comes out clean. Cool on a wire rack for 10 minutes. Remove from the pan and cool completely.

PREPARATION TIME
10 minutes

BAKING TIME
25 minutes

Maple Banana Bake

serves 4

This warm treat takes only 10 minutes to assemble. Pop it in the oven to bake while you enjoy dinner.

4	bananas, peeled and diagonally sliced
1/4	cup maple syrup
1	teaspoon lime juice
1/2	cup rolled oats
1/4	cup all-purpose flour
2	tablespoons apple juice
1	teaspoon melted butter
1/2	teaspoon vanilla
	Pinch of ground nutmeg
	Pinch of ground cinnamon
1/4	cup reduced-fat sour cream
2	tablespoons packed brown sugar

Preheat the oven to 400°. Lightly oil a shallow casserole dish.

Spread the bananas evenly in the dish. Drizzle with the maple syrup and lime juice.

In a small bowl, mix the oats, flour, apple juice, butter, vanilla, nutmeg and cinnamon. Sprinkle over the bananas.

Bake for 25 minutes, or until the topping is crisp.

In a cup, mix the sour cream and brown sugar. Serve over the bananas.

Pineapple Pound Cake

serves 8

Instant pudding and store-bought pound cake make this a quick treat when unexpected company arrives.

	PER SERVING

PER SERVING

187 calories

2.3 g. fat
(11% of calories)

0.9 g. dietary fiber

1 mg. cholesterol

194 mg. sodium

1   package (1 ounce) sugar-free vanilla instant pudding mix

1 1/2   cups skim milk

1/2   teaspoon almond extract

1   can (20 ounces) crushed pineapple in juice

1/4   cup chopped toasted almonds

1   fat-free pound cake (12 ounces)

Mandarin orange slices or sliced strawberries

PREPARATION TIME
10 minutes

Place the pudding mix in a large bowl; add the milk and almond extract. Whisk for 2 minutes. Let stand for 5 minutes to thicken.

Place the pineapple in a strainer and press with the back of a spoon to remove as much of the juice as possible; reserve the juice for another use. Fold the pineapple and almonds into the pudding.

Cut the cake into 8 slices. Spoon the pudding mixture over the slices. Top with the oranges or strawberries.

Chef's Note

For a more elegant presentation, cut the cake horizontally into 3 layers. Place 1 layer, cut side up, on a serving platter. Spread with one-third of the pudding mixture. Repeat twice to use all the cake and pudding. Decorate with the oranges or strawberries. If the layers slide while the pudding is still soft, hold them in place by spearing the cake with skewers at the corners. Chill before serving.

PREPARATION TIME
15 minutes

COOKING TIME
20 minutes

Strawberry Waffles
with Strawberry-Rhubarb Sauce

serves 4

The Dutch are given credit for introducing waffles to this country in 1796. These have a double dose of strawberries from preserves and frozen berries. During the summer, use a pint of fresh berries.

Strawberry Waffles

1¼ cups all-purpose flour

1 teaspoon baking soda

1 cup low-fat buttermilk

¼ cup all-fruit strawberry spread

2 tablespoons fat-free egg substitute

2 tablespoons canola oil

1 egg white

Strawberry-Rhubarb Sauce

1 package (10 ounces) frozen strawberries, thawed

1 cup sliced rhubarb

2 tablespoons honey

1 tablespoon grated orange rind

TO MAKE THE STRAWBERRY WAFFLES
Preheat a waffle iron according to the manufacturer's directions.

In a medium bowl, whisk together the flour and baking soda.

In a small bowl, whisk together the buttermilk, fruit spread, egg substitute and oil. Pour over the flour mixture and mix well.

In another small bowl, beat the egg white with a clean whisk until soft peaks form. Fold into the batter.

Use about ½ cup of the batter per waffle and bake according to the manufacturer's directions.

TO MAKE THE STRAWBERRY-RHUBARB SAUCE
In a 2-quart saucepan over medium heat, cook the strawberries, rhubarb, honey and orange rind for 5 minutes, or until the rhubarb is tender. Serve warm or at room temperature.

Raspberry Bread Pudding

serves 8

Here's an excellent way to use up stale bread. For variety, you may replace the raspberries with blueberries, pitted cherries or chopped peaches. You may also use other types of bread, such as whole-grain or raisin.

1½	cups skim milk
¾	cup fat-free egg substitute
½	cup honey
1	teaspoon vanilla
¼	teaspoon ground cinnamon
¼	teaspoon ground nutmeg
4	cups oat bread cubes
2	cups raspberries

In a large bowl, whisk together the milk, egg substitute, honey, vanilla, cinnamon and nutmeg. Stir in the bread and raspberries.

Coat a 2-quart casserole dish with no-stick spray. Add the bread mixture. Cover with a lid or vented plastic wrap. Microwave on medium (50% power) for 14 minutes, stirring the mixture every 3 minutes.

Cranberry Fruitcake

serves 10

This moist cake takes only a few minutes to ready for the oven. As with many other desserts in this chapter, you may vary the fruit. Try substituting pears for the apples and blueberries for the cranberries.

PREPARATION TIME
15 minutes

BAKING TIME
25 minutes

$^2/_3$	cup whole-wheat flour
$^2/_3$	cup all-purpose flour
$^1/_2$	cup rolled oats
$1^1/_2$	teaspoons baking soda
1	teaspoon ground ginger
$^1/_2$	cup fat-free egg substitute
$^1/_2$	cup honey
$^1/_3$	cup orange juice
$^1/_4$	cup canola oil
1	teaspoon vanilla
1	cup cranberries
$^3/_4$	cup shredded apples

Preheat the oven to 350°. Coat a 13" × 9" baking dish with no-stick spray.

In a large bowl, whisk together the whole-wheat flour, all-purpose flour, oats, baking soda and ginger.

In a medium bowl, whisk together the egg substitute, honey, orange juice, oil and vanilla. Pour over the flour mixture and stir until just incorporated; do not overmix. Stir in the cranberries and apples.

Spread the batter evenly in the baking dish. Bake for 20 to 25 minutes, or until a toothpick inserted in the center comes out clean. Cool on a wire rack.

Gingerbread

serves 12

Serve this old-fashioned cake plain or with fat-free whipped topping.

1 1/4	cups all-purpose flour
1	cup whole-wheat flour
1 1/2	teaspoons ground ginger
1	teaspoon baking soda
1	teaspoon ground cinnamon
1/4	teaspoon ground allspice
1	cup hot water
1/2	cup molasses
1/2	cup honey
6	tablespoons canola oil
1/4	cup fat-free egg substitute

Preheat the oven to 325°. Coat an 8" × 8" baking dish with no-stick spray.

In a large bowl, whisk together the all-purpose flour, whole-wheat flour, ginger, baking soda, cinnamon and allspice.

In a medium bowl, whisk together the water, molasses, honey, oil and egg substitute. Pour over the flour mixture and beat until smooth.

Pour the batter into the baking dish. Bake for 50 minutes, or until a toothpick inserted in the center comes out clean. Cool on a wire rack.

American Harvest Loaf

makes 1 loaf (12 wedges)

You'll be glad you spent the time baking this wonderfully flavorful and versatile bread. It freezes well and makes great toast. Cut slices into cubes and dry them for crunchy croutons to sprinkle on soups or salads.

PREPARATION TIME
15 minutes
plus 40 minutes
rising time

BAKING TIME
35 minutes

Photo on page 55

1/2	cup cracked wheat
1	cup boiling water
1	cup whole-wheat flour
1/4	cup oat bran
1/4	cup sunflower seeds
1	package quick-rise yeast
1/4	teaspoon salt
2	cups all-purpose flour
3/4	cup warm water (120°)
2	tablespoons honey

In a small bowl, mix the cracked wheat and boiling water. Let stand for 10 minutes.

In a large bowl, whisk together the whole-wheat flour, oat bran, sunflower seeds, yeast, salt and 1 cup of the all-purpose flour.

In a cup, mix the warm water and honey. Pour over the flour mixture. Add the undrained cracked wheat. Beat until the dough forms a rough-looking mass.

Turn the dough out onto a lightly floured surface and knead in enough of the remaining all-purpose flour to form a soft dough. Knead for 5 minutes.

Coat a large bowl with no-stick spray. Place the dough in the bowl. Cover with plastic wrap and allow to rise for 10 minutes. Press the dough to eliminate any air bubbles. Shape into a 12" round.

Coat a large baking sheet with no-stick spray. Place the loaf on the sheet. Mist the top with no-stick spray. Cover with plastic wrap. Let rise for 30 minutes, or until doubled in size.

Bake at 350° for 35 minutes, or until a toothpick inserted in the center comes out clean.

PREPARATION TIME
15 minutes

BAKING TIME
25 minutes

Focaccia

makes 1 loaf (8 wedges)

Focaccia is the flat bread of Italy. Before being baked, the dough is often deeply poked with a finger to hold herbs, olive oil and any number of other ingredients. Focaccia bread is generally served warm or at room temperature but never sizzling hot like pizza.

1	cup warm water (120°)
1	package quick-rise yeast
1	teaspoon honey
2½–3	cups all-purpose flour
1	tablespoon chopped fresh rosemary
1	tablespoon chopped fresh sage
1½	teaspoons salt
3	tablespoons olive oil

Preheat the oven to 400°. Coat a large baking sheet with no-stick spray.

In a large bowl, whisk together the water, yeast and honey. Whisk in 1 cup of the flour and beat until smooth. Let stand for 5 minutes.

Beat in the rosemary, sage, salt, 2 tablespoons of the oil and 1 cup of the remaining flour. Beat for 3 minutes, or until smooth. Beat in enough of the remaining flour to form a soft, sticky dough.

Turn the dough out onto a lightly floured surface and knead for 3 minutes.

Transfer to the baking sheet and shape into a 9" round about 1" thick. Brush with the remaining 1 tablespoon oil.

Bake for 20 to 25 minutes, or until golden brown.

Sweet Temptations

DELECTABLE DESSERTS
THAT ARE GOOD FOR YOU

In this chapter, we've gathered a host of luscious sweets. Some of the desserts, such as biscotti, were inspired by and borrowed from the diverse cultures that make up this country. But we've also created lots of all-American sweet traditions—like cherry pie, chocolate cake, carrot cake, cheesecake and rice pudding. Now if you're thinking that these desserts are off your eating list because they're high in fat, think again! We've reduced the fat in each and every one so you can enjoy them often.

Summertime Fruit Pizza

serves 8

What a novel way to turn a classic main course into dessert! Feel free to improvise with whatever fruit you have on hand.

PER SERVING

277 calories

5.8 g. fat
(32% of calories)

2.5 g. dietary fiber

16 mg. cholesterol

101 mg. sodium

PREPARATION TIME
10 minutes
plus 30 minutes
chilling time

BAKING TIME
12 minutes

1	cup all-purpose flour
3	tablespoons sugar
2	tablespoons finely chopped almonds
1/4	cup low-fat buttermilk
2	tablespoons canola oil
8	ounces reduced-fat cream cheese, softened
1/2	cup confectioners' sugar
1	teaspoon grated orange rind
3	kiwifruit, sliced
1	cup sliced strawberries
1	nectarine, sliced
1/2	cup apple jelly, melted

In a large bowl, whisk together the flour, sugar, and almonds. Stir in the buttermilk and oil. Form into a ball, flatten, wrap in plastic wrap and refrigerate for at least 30 minutes.

Preheat the oven to 375°. Coat a pizza pan with no-stick spray.

Unwrap the dough and place it between pieces of wax paper. Gently roll into a circle about 1/8" thick. Remove the top piece of wax paper. Invert the dough onto the pan. Remove the remaining piece of wax paper.

Bake for 12 minutes, or until lightly browned. Cool on a wire rack.

In a medium bowl, beat together the cream cheese, confectioners' sugar and orange rind. Spread over the crust. Arrange the kiwifruit, strawberries and nectarines on top. Brush with the jelly.

PREPARATION TIME
20 minutes

BAKING TIME
50 minutes

Carrot Cake

serves 16

Each bite of this cake is rich, moist and spicy. Try adding $^1/_3$ cup chopped walnuts for a different texture.

1$^3/_4$	cups all-purpose flour
1	cup whole-wheat flour
2	teaspoons baking powder
2	teaspoons baking soda
2	teaspoons ground cinnamon
1	teaspoon ground nutmeg
$^3/_4$	teaspoon ground allspice
$^1/_4$	teaspoon salt
2	eggs
4	egg whites
1	cup packed brown sugar
1	cup fat-free plain yogurt
$^1/_4$	cup canola oil
2	cups grated carrots
1	cup drained canned crushed pineapple
$^2/_3$	cup currants
8	ounces reduced-fat cream cheese, softened
1	box (16 ounces) confectioners' sugar
2	teaspoons vanilla

Preheat the oven to 325°. Coat a 13" × 9" baking dish with no-stick spray.

In a medium bowl, whisk together the all-purpose flour, whole-wheat flour, baking powder, baking soda, cinnamon, nutmeg, allspice and salt. In a large bowl, beat the eggs and egg whites with an electric mixer on medium speed until foamy. Add the brown sugar. Beat for 3 minutes. Add the yogurt and oil. Beat until creamy. On low speed, beat in the flour mixture. Gently stir in the carrots, pineapple and currants. Spread in the baking dish.

Bake for 40 to 50 minutes, or until a toothpick inserted in the center comes out clean. Cool on a wire rack.

In a large bowl, beat the cream cheese, confectioners' sugar and vanilla until smooth. Spread over the cooled cake.

Chocolate-Orange Swirl Cheesecake

serves 12

Say yes to cheesecake when it's this low in fat—and super delicious in the bargain!

PER SERVING

293 calories

7.6 g. fat
(30% of calories)

1.8 g. dietary fiber

38 mg. cholesterol

323 mg. sodium

PREPARATION TIME
10 minutes

BAKING TIME
30 minutes

1½	cups chocolate cookie crumbs
8	ounces reduced-fat cream cheese, softened
1	cup low-fat ricotta cheese
2	eggs
3	tablespoons cornstarch
1	tablespoon grated orange rind
¾	cup plus 2 tablespoons sugar
¼	cup unsweetened cocoa powder

Preheat the oven to 400°.

Coat a 9" pie plate with no-stick spray. Press the cookie crumbs evenly over the bottom and up the sides.

In a large bowl, beat together the cream cheese and ricotta until smooth. Stir in the eggs, cornstarch, orange rind and ¾ cup of the sugar.

Pour half of the mixture into another bowl. Stir in the cocoa powder and the remaining 2 tablespoons sugar. Pour into the pie plate.

Spoon the remaining cheese mixture over the top and swirl with a knife to achieve a marbleized effect.

Bake for 30 minutes, or until a knife inserted in the center comes out clean.

Chef's Note

You may substitute graham cracker crumbs for the chocolate cookie crumbs.

PREPARATION TIME
10 minutes

BAKING TIME
30 minutes

New York Cheesecake

serves 12

Reduced-fat cream cheese and a skinny cookie crust are the secrets to this light treat. For a lovely presentation, garnish with fresh fruit.

$1/3$	cup amaretti cookie crumbs
8	ounces reduced-fat cream cheese, softened
1	cup reduced-fat ricotta cheese
$1/4$	cup honey
3	tablespoons cornstarch
1	tablespoon grated orange rind
2	eggs, separated

Preheat the oven to 400°.

Coat a 9" pie plate with no-stick spray. Press the cookie crumbs evenly over the bottom and up the sides.

In a large bowl, beat together the cream cheese and ricotta until smooth. Stir in the honey, cornstarch, orange rind and egg yolks.

In a medium bowl, whip the egg whites with clean beaters until soft peaks form. Fold into the cream cheese mixture. Pour into the pie plate.

Bake for 30 minutes, or until a knife inserted in the center comes out clean.

Chef's Note
You may substitute graham cracker crumbs for the amaretti crumbs.

Sweet Temptations

Quick Chocolate Cake

serves 12

This rich-tasting snack cake has old-fashioned chocolate flavor, yet it's very light, thanks to the buttermilk. Extra pieces make great lunchbox treats.

PER SERVING

235 calories

4.9 g. fat
(18% of calories)

0.7 g. dietary fiber

27 mg. cholesterol

152 mg. sodium

1	cup all-purpose flour
1/2	cup unsweetened cocoa powder
1	teaspoon ground cinnamon
1/2	teaspoon ground nutmeg
1/2	teaspoon baking powder
1/2	teaspoon baking soda
1	cup packed brown sugar
1/2	cup applesauce
2	tablespoons canola oil
1	tablespoon vanilla
1	egg
1/2	cup low-fat buttermilk
2	egg whites
	Confectioner's sugar (optional)

PREPARATION TIME
15 minutes

BAKING TIME
30 minutes

Preheat the oven to 350°. Coat an 8" × 8" baking dish with no-stick spray.

In medium bowl, whisk together the flour, cocoa powder, cinnamon, nutmeg, baking powder and baking soda.

In a large bowl, whisk together the brown sugar, applesauce, oil, vanilla and egg. Alternately beat in the flour mixture and the buttermilk, beginning and ending with the flour mixture.

In a small bowl, whip the egg whites with clean beaters until soft peaks form. Fold into the batter. Pour into the baking dish.

Bake for 25 to 30 minutes, or until a toothpick inserted in the center comes out clean. Cool on a wire rack. Dust with confectioner's sugar (if using) before slicing.

PREPARATION TIME
25 minutes

BAKING TIME
40 minutes

Sweetheart Cherry Pie

serves 4

Who doesn't love cherry pie? This pretty, low-fat version is decorated with pastry hearts.

Cherry Filling

4	cups pitted sour cherries
1/2	cup maple syrup
3	tablespoons quick-cooking tapioca
1	teaspoon ground cinnamon

Pie Crust

1	cup cake flour
1/4	cup butter or margarine, cut into small pieces
1	egg white

TO MAKE THE CHERRY FILLING
In a 2-quart saucepan, mix the cherries, maple syrup, tapioca and cinnamon. Let stand for 5 minutes. Cook over medium heat for 10 minutes, stirring occasionally.

TO MAKE THE PIE CRUST
Preheat the oven to 400°.

Place the flour in a medium bowl. Using 2 knives, cut in the butter or margarine until the mixture resembles coarse meal. Stir in the egg white. Transfer to a lightly floured surface and knead for 30 seconds, or until smooth.

Reserve 1/4 cup of the dough. Place the remaining dough between sheets of wax paper and roll into a 9" circle. Remove the top piece of wax paper. Invert the dough onto an 8" pie plate. Remove the remaining piece of wax paper and fit the dough into the pie plate. Fold under the excess pastry and crimp the edges. Prick the bottom of the dough and bake for 10 minutes.

Roll the reserved dough between sheets of wax paper to 1/8" thickness. Using a cookie cutter, cut out hearts or other decorative shapes.

Pour the cherry filling into the pie crust and arrange the cutouts on top. Reduce the oven temperature to 350°. Bake for 30 minutes.

Chef's Note
You may use frozen sour cherries that have been thawed instead of fresh cherries.

Rustic Plum-Walnut Tart

serves 6

PER SERVING

244 calories

6.2 g. fat
(22% of calories)

1.7 g. dietary fiber

0 mg. cholesterol

123 mg. sodium

PREPARATION TIME
20 minutes

BAKING TIME
45 minutes

This free-form tart makes delicious use of beautiful late-summer plums.

Crust

1	cup all-purpose flour
1	tablespoon sugar
1/4	teaspoon salt
1/4	teaspoon ground cinnamon
2	tablespoons canola oil
3–4	tablespoons ice water

Plum Filling

4	tablespoons low-fat granola
2	tablespoons all-purpose flour
2	tablespoons chopped toasted walnuts
1/3	cup plus 1 teaspoon sugar
6	plums, quartered
1	tablespoon skim milk
2	tablespoons red currant jelly

TO MAKE THE CRUST

In a medium bowl, whisk together the flour, sugar, salt and cinnamon. Using a fork, slowly stir in the oil until the mixture is crumbly. Stir in enough of the ice water to form a dough that holds together. (It will be a little wetter than traditional pastry dough.)

Place the dough between sheets of wax paper and roll into a 12" circle. Remove the top piece of wax paper. Invert the dough onto a baking sheet. Remove the remaining piece of wax paper.

TO MAKE THE PLUM FILLING

Preheat the oven to 400°.

In a food processor, process the granola, flour, walnuts and 1/3 cup of the sugar until finely ground. Spread over the dough, leaving about a 2" border.

Decoratively arrange the plums on top of the granola mixture. Fold the dough border over the plums. Brush the milk over the dough and sprinkle with the remaining 1 teaspoon sugar.

Bake for 30 to 40 minutes, or until the crust is golden and the plums are tender. With a spatula, slide the tart onto a platter and let cool.

Melt the jelly in a 1-quart saucepan over low heat. Brush over the plums.

Oven-Puffed Pancake

serves 4

PER SERVING

185 calories

7.2 g. fat
(36% of calories)

0.4 g. dietary fiber

0 mg. cholesterol

80 mg. sodium

PREPARATION TIME
10 minutes

BAKING TIME
20 minutes

The Dutch call them pannekoeken. *You'll just call them fabulous. For the most dramatic "puff," cook the pancake in a wide pan. For a different taste, top with two chopped apples such as Red Delicious and Granny Smith before adding the brown sugar.*

3/4	cup fat-free egg substitute
1/2	cup skim milk
2	tablespoons canola oil
2	teaspoons vanilla
1	teaspoon ground nutmeg
1/2	cup all-purpose flour
2	tablespoons packed brown sugar
2	tablespoons lemon juice

Preheat the oven to 450°. Coat a large ovenproof frying pan or cast-iron skillet with no-stick spray.

In a medium bowl, whisk together the egg substitute, milk, oil, vanilla and nutmeg. Slowly whisk in the flour to form a smooth batter. Pour into the pan.

Cook over medium heat for 2 minutes to set the batter. Bake for 15 minutes. Reduce the oven temperature to 350° and bake for 5 minutes, or until puffed and golden brown.

Sprinkle with the brown sugar and lemon juice. Serve immediately.

Praline Cookie Cups

makes 8

Fill these thin, buttery, nutty cups with fresh berries or low-fat frozen yogurt.

- 1/4 cup all-purpose flour
- 1/4 cup packed brown sugar
- 2 tablespoons butter or margarine, softened
- 2 tablespoons light corn syrup
- 2 tablespoons chopped toasted hazelnuts

Preheat the oven to 375°. Coat a large baking sheet with no-stick spray.

In a medium bowl, mix the flour, brown sugar, butter or margarine, corn syrup and hazelnuts. Divide the dough into 8 pieces and form into balls.

Place the balls 3" apart on the baking sheet and press lightly to flatten.

Bake for 5 to 7 minutes, or until lightly browned.

Cool on the baking sheet for 2 minutes. Loosen gently with a spatula and drape the warm cookies over the bottoms of custard cups. Let cool.

PER CUP

93 calories

4.2 g. fat
(40% of calories)

0.3 g. dietary fiber

8 mg. cholesterol

6 mg. sodium

PREPARATION TIME
5 minutes

BAKING TIME
7 minutes

PER BISCOTTI

75 calories

2.6 g. fat
(29% of calories)

0.7 g. dietary fiber

12 mg. cholesterol

44 mg. sodium

PREPARATION TIME
10 minutes

BAKING TIME
25 minutes

Chocolate-Walnut Biscotti

makes 30

Dark and rich-tasting, these biscotti keep well in an air-tight container or in the freezer. They are especially good dunked in espresso.

1	cup all-purpose flour
1/2	cup sugar
1/4	cup unsweetened cocoa powder
1/2	teaspoon baking powder
1/4	teaspoon baking soda
1/4	teaspoon salt
1	egg
1	egg white
1 1/2	teaspoons vanilla
2	ounces bittersweet chocolate, chopped
1/4	cup chopped toasted walnuts

Preheat the oven to 350°. Coat an 11" × 7" baking dish with no-stick spray.

In a large bowl, whisk together the flour, sugar, cocoa powder, baking powder, baking soda and salt.

In a medium bowl, whisk together the egg, egg white and vanilla. Pour over the flour mixture and stir well. Stir in the chocolate and walnuts.

Press the dough into the baking dish. Bake for 25 minutes, or until firm. Transfer to a wire rack and cut into 30 fingers. Cool before serving.

Chef's Note
To toast nuts, spread them on a baking sheet and bake at 400° for 10 minutes, or until lightly browned and fragrant. Do not let them burn.

Mocha-Almond Biscotti

makes 30

PER BISCOTTI

73 calories

2.2 g. fat
(26% of calories)

0 g. dietary fiber

11 mg. cholesterol

52 mg. sodium

Mild chocolate and light almond flavor come together nicely in this crunchy cookie. Great for dunking.

PREPARATION TIME
10 minutes

BAKING TIME
25 minutes

1¼	cups all-purpose flour
½	cup sugar
½	teaspoon baking powder
¼	teaspoon baking soda
¼	teaspoon salt
1	egg
1	egg white
1	teaspoon vanilla
½	teaspoon almond extract
1	tablespoon instant coffee powder
1	tablespoon warm water
1	ounce unsweetened chocolate, melted
⅓	cup slivered toasted almonds

Preheat the oven to 350°. Coat an 11" × 7" baking dish with no-stick spray.

In a large bowl, whisk together the flour, sugar, baking powder, baking soda and salt.

In a medium bowl, whisk together the egg, egg white, vanilla and almond extract. In a cup, dissolve the coffee in the water; stir into the bowl. Stir in the chocolate. Pour over the flour mixture and stir well. Stir in the almonds.

Press the dough into the baking dish. Bake for 25 minutes, or until firm. Transfer to a wire rack and cut into 30 fingers. Cool before serving.

PREPARATION TIME
5 minutes

COOKING TIME
35 minutes

Mandarin Rice Pudding

serves 6

Here's an easy rice pudding that gets Asian flair from mandarin oranges and crystallized ginger. For an even more intriguing flavor, start with an aromatic rice, such as basmati. This pudding is good warm or chilled.

1	cup rice
2	teaspoons canola oil
2	cups water
1/4	teaspoon ground cinnamon
1	can (15 ounces) evaporated skim milk
1	cup drained and chopped mandarin oranges
2	tablespoons minced crystallized ginger
2	tablespoons toasted almonds

In a 3-quart saucepan over medium heat, stir the rice and oil for 3 minutes, or until glossy. Stir in the water and cinnamon. Bring to a boil. Cover, reduce the heat to medium-low and simmer for 20 minutes, or until all the liquid has been absorbed.

Stir in the milk. Cook, stirring often, for 10 minutes. Stir in the oranges, ginger and almonds.

Index

Underscored page references indicate Chef's Notes. **Boldface** references indicate photographs.

Conversion Chart

These equivalents have been slightly rounded to make measuring easier.

VOLUME MEASUREMENTS

U.S.	Imperial	Metric
¼ tsp	–	1.25 ml
½ tsp	–	2.5 ml
1 tsp	–	5 ml
1 Tbsp	–	15 ml
2 Tbsp (1 oz)	1 fl oz	30 ml
¼ cup (2 oz)	2 fl oz	60 ml
⅓ cup (3 oz)	3 fl oz	80 ml
½ cup (4 oz)	4 fl oz	120 ml
⅔ cup (5 oz)	5 fl oz	160 ml
¾ cup (6 oz)	6 fl oz	180 ml
1 cup (8 oz)	8 fl oz	240 ml

WEIGHT MEASUREMENTS

U.S.	Metric
1 oz	30 g
2 oz	60 g
4 oz (¼ lb)	115 g
5 oz (⅓ lb)	145 g
6 oz	170 g
7 oz	200 g
8 oz (½ lb)	230 g
10 oz	285 g
12 oz (¾ lb)	340 g
14 oz	400 g
16 oz (1 lb)	455 g
2.2 lb	1 kg

LENGTH MEASUREMENTS

U.S.	Metric
¼"	0.6 cm
½"	1.25 cm
1"	2.5 cm
2"	5 cm
4"	11 cm
6"	15 cm
8"	20 cm
10"	25 cm
12" (1')	30 cm

PAN SIZES

U.S.	Metric
8" cake pan	20 × 4-cm sandwich or cake tin
9" cake pan	23 × 3.5-cm sandwich or cake tin
11" × 7" baking pan	28 × 18-cm baking pan
13" × 9" baking pan	32.5 × 23-cm baking pan
2-qt rectangular baking dish	30 × 19-cm baking dish
15" × 10" baking pan	38 × 25.5-cm baking pan (Swiss roll tin)
9" pie plate	22 × 4 or 23 × 4-cm pie plate
7" or 8" springform pan	18 or 20-cm springform or loose-bottom cake tin
9" × 5" loaf pan	23 × 13-cm or 2-lb narrow loaf pan or pâté tin
1½-qt casserole	1.5-l casserole
2-qt casserole	2-l casserole

TEMPERATURES

Fahrenheit	Centigrade	Gas
140°	60°	–
160°	70°	–
180°	80°	–
225°	110°	–
250°	120°	½
300°	150°	2
325°	160°	3
350°	180°	4
375°	190°	5
400°	200°	6
450°	230°	8
500°	260°	–